MANAGEMENT
DISEASES
AND
DISORDERS

How to Identify and Treat Dysfunctional Managerial Behavior

Steven A. Danley
and Peter Hughes Ph.D., CPA

ISBN: 978-1-4834-5456-6 (sc)
ISBN: 978-1-4834-5457-3 (e)

Library of Congress Control Number: 2016911637

Because of the dynamic nature of the Internet, any web addresses or links contained in this book may have changed
since publication and may no longer be valid. The views expressed in this work are solely those of the author and do
not necessarily reflect the views of the publisher, and the publisher hereby disclaims any responsibility for them.

Any people depicted in stock imagery provided by Thinkstock are models,
and such images are being used for illustrative purposes only.
Certain stock imagery © Thinkstock.

Lulu Publishing Services rev. date: 09/08/2016

For health and sanity in the workplace

Contents

Part 2: Culture- or System-Based Diseases and Disorders

Preface

A crown is placed over our heads that for the rest of our lives we are trying to grow tall enough to wear. — *Howard Thurman*

I was searching the Internet one day and came across a medical book that was an almanac of diseases and disorders. I had one of those aha moments. As an organizational and performance audit practitioner with more than thirty years of experience, as well as a former human resources director, I realized that there are management diseases and disorders that, to my knowledge, have never been collected, categorized, and made available for easy reference.

Suddenly, a faucet of analogies between medicine and management opened up and began to flow. Management does indeed have diseases and disorders. They may be chronic or acute, contagious or noncontagious, life-threatening or a nuisance, easy or more difficult to treat, visibly ugly or hidden under the surface, and so on.

I called my acronym-endowed (i.e., highly educated and credentialed) friend and colleague Dr. Peter Hughes to get his take on the idea and to enlist his support if he thought it was a worthwhile endeavor. To my great pleasure, he jumped in with both feet, seeing the need for and the value of the initiative. Our efforts have since expanded into multiple outlets—one of them being this book. As we shared our ideas with trusted contributors, we were met with universal recognition of the need for this effort.

It is clear, although not so well recognized, that management and leadership issues are just as significant as physical maladies—in some cases, they directly affect our personal health. After all, most people spend the vast amount of their waking hours at work, and for many their mental, emotional, and physical well-being are directly related to how their work life is progressing. This is not surprising, since one's economic capability and at least part of one's self-esteem comes from work.

Therefore, from both an organizational and a personal-health standpoint, it is imperative that we understand the diseases and disorders of management. *Management Diseases and Disorders* is dedicated to providing an initial effort at formally identifying, consolidating, analyzing, and suggesting cures for these maladies. Its motives are pure. No organizational leader will make it out of this life without contracting something. We have to understand our maladies if we ever hope to heal them and thereby improve our organizational and personal health. That is a tough task, given that human nature consistently gets in the way and makes eradication essentially impossible.

Our hope is that this book is just the beginning. It is by no means a definitive listing of management diseases and disorders. We encourage others to contribute and augment the offerings through our website (www.managementdiseasesanddisorders.com). The goal is to acknowledge the management issues we face, identify their root causes, understand their significance in achieving an effective and efficient organization, and assist in the prescription and implementation of useful treatments.

Writing this book has taken us on an amazing journey. It involved a purging of our direct observations and a documentation of management practices we have seen over a combined seventy years in the workplace. In our work assignments, we have been required to conduct a vast amount of research to verify field conditions. In this case, researching others' work was less necessary, as the validation was direct, firsthand witnessing of events and outcomes. As you read this book, you will be amazed at how it will trigger flashbacks of specific people, times, and events.

The entire writing experience has been filled with all the aspects of a good drama, eliciting both laughter and tears. The process was exhilarating, cathartic, and at times difficult. It brought back both good and bad memories of epic and valiant successes and devastating betrayals of confidence and trust. It is a book not just about leadership and management but also about life and how we choose to lead it—who we are and who we want to become in our daily work pursuits.

While recognizing the seriousness of this effort, we have tried to convey our ideas with thoughtful, sound, and yet artfully entertaining entries. We want you to consider and reflect purposefully, hoping that you delight in the twists and turns of phrases, explanations, examples, and stories. We hope you enjoy the read and use it to better your leadership skills and the quality of your workplace.

Book Structure

The listing of management diseases and disorders is divided into personality based and culture or system based. These main categories are further divided as follows:

- personality based (originating from individual managers)
  - personal deficiencies—deficiencies related to identity, ego, or self-esteem
  - interpersonal deficiencies—difficulty establishing and maintaining adequate interpersonal relationships at work
  - behavioral deficiencies
    - fear based
    - self-interest based

- skill based
- culture or system based (institutionalized conditions)
  - organizational integrity deficiencies—deficiencies in building and maintaining an ethical work culture
  - strategic foundation deficiencies—deficiencies in the establishment of effective vision, mission, goal, and value statements for the organization, including deficiencies in building an effective and efficient organizational structure
  - personnel management deficiencies—deficiencies in the supervision and management of an organization's human resources
  - process deficiencies—deficiencies in organizational processes for the efficient and effective production of goods and/or services
  - resource management deficiencies—deficiencies in managing an organization's funds, buildings, equipment, etc.

Each management disease/disorder is a separate entry comprised of the following:

- definition of condition
- healthy and normal function
- causes of dysfunction
- risk to the organization
- symptoms and signs
- diagnostic analysis[1]
- progression and impact
- prognosis
- treatment or cure

These management diseases and disorders are essentially a first-edition "most wanted" list, offering a photo (definition of condition), profile of characteristics, potential treatments for each, and a case study to illustrate the disease or disorder described. The inspiration for the creation of the work-related case studies are from our own experiences and from events occurring in the news. These studies were invented so that all characters, companies and scenarios depicted are fictitious, and no similarity or entities, living or deceased, was intended or should be inferred.

—SD & PH(d), pellucid prospectors of pandemic pestilence with pith and probity, and hopefully a splash of panache

---

[1] DSM criteria from a chart entitled 'DSM-IV and DSM-5 Criteria for the Personality Disorders', obtained from www.psi.uba.or/academica/.../psicologia/.../dsm.pdf, was used as a reference and source for some of the questions in the "Diagnostic Analysis" section of some individual management diseases/disorders.

Acknowledgments

This book would have not been possible without the unwavering support and assistance of a number of quality people from numerous walks of life who were glad to assist. We would like to particularly acknowledge Dr. Bryan Crow and Tom Danley—the best people we know. They are living proof that the good guys can still have an impact on society.

A special thanks to Lulu's publishing staff for their outstanding editing suggestions and guidance through the publishing process.

Lastly, with gratitude and love, we would like to acknowledge the ever-present and stabilizing force our wives have provided throughout our work years, which, on many occasions, unfortunately impacted our personal lives. We would not have made it without your support.

Introduction

At forty-four years of age, after I finished my twenty-second season of NCAA and high school basketball officiating, my wife and I decided to splurge and take a ten-day vacation to Bora Bora. It was a fabulous trip. We jet-skied, scuba-dived (with far too many sharks), took island tours, slept in, and ate heartily. A few short weeks later, I was in the emergency room having a cardiac stent placed in my left anterior descending artery, which was more than 95 percent occluded. I was fortunate to be alive.

I had no family history of heart disease, was not overweight, was in tremendous physical shape, and had a good home life. My doctors were surprised and had few answers as to why this had happened. The only area of my life that was in a churn was work. For the previous two years, I had been directed to testify as a witness in a nasty harassment case. The mishandling of the case was so egregious that I couldn't shake the emotional ramifications, and I internalized much of my frustration.

Much of what I'd believed about my organization had been turned upside down. Since the organization's 1994 bankruptcy, I knew it had slowly been changing for the worse, but I didn't realize how much, because I was not yet in the inner circle as an executive. For the first time, I saw behind the curtain. It was disheartening.

Examinations

It's commonly recognized as a good idea to get an annual physical from the family internist. This once-a-year examination is a barometer of our personal health (mind, body, and spirit) that proactively allows us to address anything that needs attention before it becomes a serious condition. The same can be said for work. The organizational mind is its executives, the body is its operational capabilities, and the spirit is the culture in which its employees operate.

Just as no one wants to be sick, no one wants to work for a sick organization. The same type of effort that goes into maintaining our personal health can be applied toward the health of an organization. After all, an organization is an inanimate object made up of living organisms called employees.

Common Concerns

A common disappointment in life is when outward beauty far exceeds the quality of the inner personality. It is indeed sublime when the contents of the package are as nice as its wrapping.

The same holds true for organizations. The corporate history of the United States is rife with examples of organizations being pronounced healthy by Wall Street and shortly thereafter needing a pallbearer. For some people, beauty is only skin deep; for some organizations, finances are only paper deep.

This facade enables covert hypocrisy in an organization. If this becomes a chronic condition, the organization may appear very shiny and clean on the outside as it proclaims all the right things. On the inside, though, a select few are scheming, conniving, and politicizing for their own benefit. The reality of any organization can be found in the personal behavior and values of its leaders. Sick organizations are virtual petri dishes for management diseases and disorders.

Why Be Healthy?

Good health is such a fundamental priority that this question may seem unnecessary. Surely this is so from a personal-health standpoint, but what about from an organization's point of view? Consider the following questions: Do you feel the same level of concern for the health of the organization as you have for yourself? Would it be okay if you did extremely well at work but the organization floundered? How emotionally tied are you to your organization and its success or failure?

There are at least five spectacular reasons why we should be just as concerned about organizational health as we are about personal health. These include the following:

1. *A healthy organization establishes a mutually beneficial bottom line.* Typically, when a company is doing well, so are its employees. If the key leaders are healthy in terms of honesty, integrity, and competence, the organization will be healthy as well.
2. *A healthy organization contributes to a physically and mentally healthier workforce.* Considering most of us spend the vast majority of our waking hours at or thinking about work, a better-run organization translates into less stress.
3. *A healthy organization creates sustainability.* Both the company and its employees want to know that the business is a sustainable, ongoing entity. To be sustainable, a company needs to be healthy. To be healthy, it needs to know its performance numbers. To know its numbers, it needs to care. To care, it needs to have character. This concern is not just for today. Tomorrow's executives want to work for an organization that educates, motivates, and inspires them. They will avoid working for an organization that is inefficiently or ineffectively operated, hypocritically managed, or unappreciative of their efforts.[2]

---

[2] Micah Soloman, "2015 Is the Year of the Millennial Customer: 5 Key Traits These 80 Million Customers Share," *Forbes,* December 29, 2014; Katherine Reynolds Lewis, "Everything You Need to Know About Your Millennial Co-workers," *Fortune,* June 25, 2015; Terri Klass and Judy Lindenberger, "Characteristics of Millennials in the Workplace," *Business Know How,* accessed January 20, 2016, http://www.businessknowhow.com/manage/millenials.htm.

4. *A healthy organization is a catalyst for a civil society.* Private business is one of the fundamental pillars of a civilized society. Without free enterprise, we are not free people. If we are unable to earn a living, to purchase goods and services, and to have meaningful work, the government will attempt to provide all of these things. And if government provides these things, neither it nor we will be free.

5. *A healthy organization gives good and talented employees an opportunity to compete.* Sometimes the most disadvantaged employee in a sick organization is the healthy or "good" person. This is because the working sick are not easy to detect as they mask their true nature and intentions, while the good are transparent and their actions match their words. Without an adequate understanding of this dark side, ethical employees may be confused and disheartened, and hibernate into a self-preservation mode. The authors intend for this book to provide good and healthy employees with the ability to more readily spot and remedy the common illnesses that afflict managers before these become prolific or fatal.

PART

1

Personality-Based
Diseases and Disorders

Chapter 1

Personal Deficiencies

The Egomaniac

- Divinity Complex
- Lack of Self-Examination
- Managerial Addiction
- Abusive Insecurity

Divinity Complex

The belief that when one is hired as an executive, one becomes infinitely more skilled and perhaps infallible.

Healthy and Normal Function

The board of directors and CEO participate in open and legitimate processes to find the best-qualified candidate for each executive position based on documented skills and abilities. The executive hired is a well-balanced individual who understands his or her strengths and weaknesses, and engages the best and brightest to improve the organization.

Causes of Dysfunction

- the belief that getting the job proves that one is the best-qualified person, and therefore smarter and more skilled than anyone else
- the belief that one must play the part whether one has the goods or not
- an inaccurate belief that one's selection as an executive is a result of the will of God

Risk to the Organization

Quality executives never entertain the notion that they become divine upon appointment. If nothing else, their families bring them back down to earth on a daily basis. After all, a real God can't be appointed. Good executives know that there are all kinds of reasons people land the top jobs, and many of those reasons have nothing to do with logic or skill. In fact, in some cases, executives get the job precisely because they have a "vitamin E" (ethics) deficiency.

Under-qualified executives who do buy into this false self-image set themselves and the organization up for failure. This viewpoint screams inadequacy. Milking the self-deception screams mental instability; internalizing it ensures failure. The risks to the organization increase with each progressive layer applied.

Symptoms and Signs

- acting smarter and more qualified than anyone else in the organization
- hiring unqualified people to ensure that one is indeed smarter than everybody else
- jealously standing guard for those who hired one; after all, if one is infallible, those who begat one must be infallible as well
- sharing one's world philosophy or pontificating on any topic
- lying and manipulating staff to accomplish desired ends
- feeling that one can just pronounce something and it instantly becomes truth
- belief that one is unaccountable to others
- belief that one must be obeyed under any and all circumstances

Diagnostic Analysis

- What happens when someone disagrees with the divine?
- Have there been noticeable personality and idiosyncratic behavioral changes since this individual was promoted?
- Has there been an increase in ethical compromises?
- Is there any structure for holding this individual accountable?
- Does the individual show any remorse for dishonesty and subterfuge?
- Does the individual value loyalty more than skill or character?

Progression and Impact

This is not simply a matter of feeling good about oneself because one was selected to a top position in the organization. It's about falsely believing that one acquired new skills and talents immediately following one's selection, and that one is now more than up to the challenge of making critical resource and policy decisions in previously uncharted areas of expertise.

It's easy to fall victim to the belief that one underestimated oneself prior to selection but now has been set straight about one's real value to the organization. After all, once the job is obtained, everyone says the right selection was made. After each decision, the majority agree that the decision was the absolute right call. When anyone disagrees, the affected executive subtly reiterates his/her viewpoint, and nearly all concern vanishes. For the more critical, just a look over the glasses makes objections disappear.

However, being a false deity eventually has its downside. Soon gaps between verbiage and actual results become apparent. Soliloquies are revealed as gobbledygook. The fine wine of political manipulation becomes the harsh whine of a blown organizational transmission. Ultimately, the Midas touch becomes Medusa-like, and the halo fits more like a noose.

Prognosis

Having an executive with a divinity complex ensures unmet expectations. As in marriage, the only thing worse than being single is having the wrong spouse. An executive who is not as qualified as he or she thinks marks the start of a long uphill journey without sufficient fuel to make it to the top.

Treatment or Cure

Hire executives who are qualified for the job in all respects. Have the executive utilize an accountability group or personal counsel to receive advice on a variety of issues and maintain the ethical health of the organization. Demonstrate to the executive how his or her behavior is hurting their chances for success at work, and be direct about the consequences of not improving personal deficiencies. Ensure the executive is amenable to healthy and respectful debate.

Case Study

Bully Flop

Camille, a new executive, was hired despite a dubious background featuring numerous scandals. In one of her previous jobs, she had accused a high-ranking official of ordering her to falsify company records. What wasn't said was that Camille did not have the courage to disobey the order and only complained after the investigation started. Additionally, in a separate private venture, Camille was under investigation for questionable economic deals. Although a bulletproof case could not be made, it was abundantly clear that she was considered a very shady person by a lot of folks.

Upon taking her new job, Camille threatened her supervisor if he failed to meet her organizational demands. She also clumsily and maliciously fired a few longtime employees from her office and harassed another employee to hire a personal friend. Later, in an attempt to acquire additional power and influence, Camille began to manufacture false information about employees and present this information to the media and at public meetings in an illegitimate attempt to suggest she was a vanguard for the public.

Camille also felt entirely comfortable reaching agreements with other company executives on a variety of issues only to take diametrically opposed actions, often as early as the next day. Truth appeared to be irrelevant to Camille; the only thing that seemed to matter was increasing her power and influence at the expense of anyone who stood in her way.

Although unblessed by a lack of experience and managerial skill, Camille considered herself immune from accountability and free to pillage the company to her desired ends. As a result of her actions, the organization was in constant turmoil, and no one wanted to work with her or her organization.

Lack of Self-Examination

The difficulty or inability to adequately examine and purposefully reflect on one's motives, values, and behaviors in the workplace.

Healthy and Normal Function

Healthy individuals take stock of their motives, decisions, and actions to determine if these align with accepted ethical standards. When harm or offense is done, they apologize and take specific actions to ameliorate the impact of the offense, and follow it up by pursuing personal change.

Causes of Dysfunction

There can be many reasons why those in leadership positions have difficulty owning up to their motives, values, and resulting behaviors. Some are psychological and some are pragmatic in nature. Examples include the following:

- *Personality disorders based in fear*—Although we are not psychologists or psychiatrists, we have dealt directly with our share of deeply disturbed individuals in the workplace. *Disaffectation*[3] is a psychological disorder in which a person does not allow himself or herself to admit to having severe motivational or behavioral deficiencies because doing so could irreparably damage an unmerited sense of integrity and identity. In essence, people with the disorder will not or cannot take responsibility for certain kinds of behaviors because it would be too painful and could significantly damage their psychological stability. This is an ironic, self-absorbed reaction, as potential pain to the perpetrator trumps the actual pain of the victim.
- *Sense of destiny*—Many with this disorder see themselves as the beginning and the end: "Of course I'm in management, it's my destiny." As such, there can be no other purpose than to relentlessly pursue what they know to be true: "I am the most important person in the universe (at least in this organization) and deserve to be treated as such. Anyone who disagrees must be discarded so that I might fulfill my destiny."
- *Fear that admitting flaws would limit options*—Not allowing oneself to contemplate the moral and ethical profundities of bad behavior makes it increasingly possible to imagine and follow through on malicious acts, or to subsequently blame others for the consequences of one's behavior.

---

[3] J. McDougall, "The 'Dis-Affected' Patient: Reflections on Affect Pathology," *Psychoanalytic Quarterly* 53: 386-409.

- *Belief that admitting flaws would be a competitive disadvantage*—One way to rationalize bad behavior is to conclude that no one else is holding back in taking whatever measures are necessary to reach their goals. Ergo, the individual believes that "if no one else is balancing the weights on the moral scale, then I have no obligation to do so. In fact, if I do, it will put me in a disadvantageous position."

Risk to the Organization

Having individuals with this disorder in leadership positions puts a company in an extremely precarious situation. Typically, such leaders have few if any boundaries to curb or shape their behaviors. They can't or choose not to accept responsibility for the harm their actions cause to employees and the organization. They may see the pain on a person's face, but they do not see what they did to cause the pain. As a result, they do not learn from their mistakes, as these are not seen as mistakes.

Such actions will inevitably be repeated many times over in different circumstances and with different people. Managers or executives with this deficiency are just as likely to manufacture false information to damage a person's reputation as they are to dig up actual dirt for the same purpose. These behaviors place the organization at risk for a compliance violation or lawsuit. The organization will lose many of these cases, because executives with this disorder don't typically cover their tracks, as they do not view what they are doing as wrong.

Symptoms and Signs

- willingness to step over anyone to reach a desired goal
- unwillingness to accept feedback
- multiple demonstrations of incongruent behavior, such as initial gregariousness with employees followed by undeserved slights, or repeated displays of cooperation and consensus followed by actions that do the opposite of what was agreed upon
- replacement of talented employees with sycophants
- failure to admit mistakes unless it helps obtain immediate forgiveness for a significant transgression
- irrational anger toward wronged employees who have trouble immediately forgiving or allowing one back into a position of trust
- no effort to hide egregious behavior
- constant and false references to oneself as an ethical and upright person

Diagnostic Analysis

- Is the individual unwilling or unable to admit any deficiencies?

- Does the individual demonstrate extreme discomfort and even walk out when confronted by a supervisor?
- Does the individual lack the ability to recognize his or her or other's feelings or emotional cues?
- Is there a lack of remorse for behaviors that inflict unwarranted pain on coworkers?
- Does the individual focus on personal gain at the expense of organizational benefit?
- Does the individual routinely lie in any situation?

Progression and Impact

When those in leadership positions are incapable of honest self-assessment, they do not default to decency. One major obstacle to identifying this type of employee is that many times they are gregarious people who like to hang out and be noticed in a crowd. They tell jokes and stories and usually have a boisterous laugh. A bigger obstacle to identification, however, is disbelief that someone can be this bad while seeming so nice on the surface. Initial slights are thought to be misunderstandings; follow-up slights are thought to be differences in opinion; malicious behavior is initially chalked up as a bad start once the person apologizes (insincerely).

If this type of employee is misdiagnosed or not dealt with quickly and aggressively, it is analogous to letting a rattlesnake roam loose in one's house. One's patience and willingness to give the person the benefit of the doubt will ultimately make one a rattle-snack. This type of employee depends upon delayed reaction and typically uses it to render others incapable of fighting back once they realize the danger of the situation.

Prognosis

In acute and chronic cases, this condition may not be salvageable, particularly if it is contracted by the CEO or a key executive. In less severe cases, expect the organization to experience significant turmoil and losses in productivity.

Treatment or Cure

Unfortunately, for those employees who refuse to "take their medicine," you cannot fix the situation as they see nothing wrong with themselves. Whatever is wrong cannot be addressed at work. In these extreme cases, a company is not a hospital and does not have sufficient restraints to contain such an individual. Inform these individuals of their performance or behavioral deficiencies and closely monitor their progress. If immediate improvements are not made, remove that person from management. For less severe cases, devote significant supervisory attention or bring in an executive coach to work with the individual to first recognize the condition, and then to ascertain their willingness to address their issues.

Case Study

It's Not My Fault

A high school basketball coach had difficulty performing the major functions of his job. In one situation, the coach had unusual difficulty maintaining his balance and made profane statements at a team function. In response to the incident, the coach refused to admit he had a problem. Instead, the coach blamed his problems on personal stress, lack of sleep, and medications he was taking.

At a later date, the coach was accused of arriving at team facilities stoned. It was also alleged that the coach may have been intoxicated during games, practices, and while the team was traveling. He was first placed on paid leave and then fired from his job.

In response, the coach filed a lawsuit against the school district—claiming, among other things, employer discrimination on the basis of having a disability. The school district disputed much of the coach's claims, describing them as wild exaggerations. The district emphasized that it had an obligation to provide a safe environment for its athletes and therefore responded appropriately. The case is still in litigation.

Managerial Addiction

The undeterred pursuit and resulting addiction to managerial enticements like fame, power, money, adulation, and territory.

Healthy and Normal Function

Employees are able to responsibly enjoy healthy doses of managerial enticements while being open to receiving counseling and assistance as necessary and appropriate.

Causes of Dysfunction

- addictive personality
- desire to control
- desire to feed the ego
- desire for a more comfortable life
- the wrong priorities
- desire to deaden the pain of everyday life with possessions and recognition
- belief that "someone has to be on top, and it might as well be me"

Risk to the Organization

The risk to the organization from this disease increases with each step up the ladder of an addictive personality. Addiction inspires extreme actions in an effort to satisfy desires at any cost. There is also the substantial risk that the addictive behaviors of one person will cause a chain reaction and result in a run on the rewards structure of an organization.

After all, there are only so many rewards to go around. If multiple sycophants are turned loose, there will be fewer managers tending to the achievement of the mission of the organization. The large sucking sound heard in this environment is the soul of the organization going down the drain.

Symptoms and Signs

- throwing fellow employees under the bus as necessary
- manipulating opportunities to receive praise

- constantly checking the vacancy report for promotional opportunities and not caring if a plane crashed with all the top executives on board as long as it opens up some rungs on the ladder
- volunteering to assist those at the top with any personal needs
- feeling depressed if not complimented at least once a day
- panic attack if someone else is promoted
- vastly overdressing the part

Diagnostic Analysis

- When you justly remove a perk—for example, take away responsibility, exclude him or her from a meeting on an important topic, praise other people, deliver a standard performance evaluation and minimal raise, or imply that the individual is not perfect—does the individual have a strong negative reaction?
- How many ways and times does the individual try to gratuitously contact executive management during the work day?
- If asked to critique other employees, does he or she have difficulty saying anything complimentary?
- If you gave the individual a blank check, what would he or she do with it?
- How does the individual act on the spur of the moment in response to immediately obtaining a wanted enticement?
- Does the individual engage in risky and potentially self-damaging behaviors without regard for the consequences?
- Are there unstable emotional reactions and frequent mood changes?

Progression and Impact

We all have inappropriate or misplaced desires for things that are not good for either us or our organization. The key to taming these desires is identifying them, making better choices over time, and developing healthier habits. Of course, this is easier said than done, particularly if the desired substance presents itself for the taking.

Managerial enticements like fame, power, and money are just as addictive as alcohol, drugs, or sex. Once addicted, an individual finds it very hard to do without a fix. Some addicts are willing to engage in scorched-earth behaviors to get another chance at that euphoric rush. The more these tendencies can be subdued or limited to lower levels of an organization, the less impact they will have. The farther a person with addictive behaviors moves up in the organization, the greater the carnage and wake of trampled employees who become a means to an end.

Prognosis

If not addressed, past doses of the enticement will not be sufficient, resulting in an escalation of bad behavior. The increasing redirection of company resources and time to pursue personal gain will come at the expense of organization's bottom line.

Treatment or Cure

- Provide formal training once an employee reaches a certain level in the organization that includes recognition and discussion of the accompanying negative enticements.
- Establish an accountability structure, perhaps to include making available a mentor or executive coach.
- As early as possible, identify and discuss potential problems with those who gravitate to or express a desire to pursue these enticements.
- Share recent examples of how executives have flamed out because they were unable to control their addictive tendencies.
- Ensure a sensible and methodical pace of progression for up-and-comers rather than moving people to the top before they are ready.
- Ensure that management/executives take real vacations during which they completely detach from the organization.

Case Study

Political Junkie

Austin was a political junkie who rode the coattails of the power elite to a top management position. Austin was intelligent but also manipulative and devious. Despite a weak resume, he maximized his value to the power elite through flattery and subservience. In return for unmerited promotions, Austin did the bidding of his benefactors.

As Austin slithered up the organizational ladder, his ethical weaknesses resulted in intermittent outbursts of trouble, which were conveniently minimized and resulted in little if any disciplinary action. However, at times, his behaviors were so brazen that there was substantial negative publicity. In these circumstances, Austin would hibernate and then reappear as other important jobs became available. Those who supervised Austin tried to navigate his political connections and contain, as best they could, his behavior.

Austin did demonstrate some value with his ability to provide advice to supervisors about how to deal with the power elite—putting in a good word for them and allowing them to gain recognition and, at times, additional job accouterments. By pursuing this strategy and being willing to step on people who got in the way, Austin eventually reached the top echelon of the organization without the necessary experience, humility, or ethics.

As it was believed Austin was generally untouchable, this promotion caused considerable damage to the organization. Austin's lack of a legitimate skill set kept him from being able to proactively identify significant problems or manage sufficient resolutions. Despite Austin's obvious addictive behaviors and the resulting chaos these behaviors created, to this day he still retains his assignment.

Abusive Insecurity

The tendency to denigrate employees after they experience a significant success in order to keep them humble, fearful, and dependent.

Healthy and Normal Function

Leadership praises and recognizes all employees for a job well done. After all, if subordinates do well, the executive team also reaps the benefits.

Causes of Dysfunction

The primary cause of this disorder is the deep-seated insecurity of a boss who cannot allow anyone to believe he or she could be replaced. It comes about when persons with significant insecurity issues are placed in positions of authority. Depending upon the level and visibility of the assignment, insecure executives typically cannot allow themselves to be viewed as anything less than perfect because that only exacerbates their insecurity. Every tick less than perfect makes it increasingly possible that they could be replaced, because in their mind, they believe they really never deserved the position in the first place.

Risk to the Organization

This type of behavior is self-defeating for both the boss and the organization. The boss's actions discourage employees from trying to succeed at a higher level and encourage them to leave the organization. If employees stay, they may be so demoralized that they never fully recover, ceasing to perform at high initiative and productivity levels. In addition, depending upon the extent of the abuse and the degree of humiliation meted out, there may be legitimate concern that an employee will assault the boss.

Symptoms and Signs

- employees are silent on important issues due to fear of a negative reaction
- calling an employee who has had a major success into the office to severely degrade him or her on an unrelated issue

- employees who are fearful of succeeding in a significant manner or prefer not to receive recognition for their successes
- grotesquely inflated flattery given to the boss
- making talented employees suddenly and inexplicably lose their confidence
- verbal hostility and thoughts of retribution by staff after undeserved verbal beatings

Diagnostic Analysis

- Are staff members subjected to consistent and routine undeserved verbal chastisements after a significant success?
- Are team successes exclusively attributed to the boss?
- Have the best staff members been quitting abruptly? What do they say in exit interviews?
- Do staff members show a lack of initiative or make recommendations based on the fear of blame if things don't work out?
- Do employees show intense dislike or hatred of the boss?
- Does the boss exhibit consistent hypersensitivity to criticism, blame, or minor slights and insults?

Progression and Impact

If this personality disorder is not recognized and addressed, the organization slowly becomes a tinderbox of on-edge emotions ready to ignite. Eventually, no one of any real talent and confidence stays with the organization. In addition, the organization becomes widely known for its tyrant, which keeps any new talent from seeking employment.

Prognosis

The effects of long-term exposure to this disorder are organizational anger, paralysis, and eventual nonproduction. The true irony is that by behaving in this manner, the boss finally makes his or her worst fear a reality.

Treatment or Cure

Preliminary treatment may include the hiring of an executive coach to ascertain the reasons for and extent of the boss's pathology to determine if there is any chance for reform. If this does not work, options include moving the boss out of management, reassigning him or her to a job that does not have supervisory responsibilities, or in extreme cases, termination.

Case Study

Unlikeable, That's What You Are

Tim was a well-qualified employee who had been promoted to an executive position. Within a week of his promotion, Tim's boss, Tina, called him into her office to cancel Tim's vacation, without concern for the fact that his planned international trip had been prepaid. Tina said that she was cancelling the vacation because Tim was too new to his position to be able to effectively deal with a critical project. Tina would have to handle it, and that meant Tim would be needed to run day-to-day operations.

There were other executives who could have run the day-to-day operations on a temporary basis, but Tina specifically wanted Tim to have the impression that although he was just promoted, he wasn't talented enough to be trusted with his new assignment. While cancelling the vacation, Tina said, "I'm sorry, Tim, you're just not competent enough yet to handle this critical assignment. Tell your wife when you get better at your job, you'll be able to take that vacation in the future."

Tina was eventually promoted to company headquarters, where her insecurity was on display to her superiors on a daily basis. Shortly thereafter, Tina unexpectedly left the organization and never stayed in touch with anyone.

Chapter 2

Interpersonal Deficiencies

The Abuser

- Abusive Expectations
- Lack of Shame
- The Aphrodisiac of Leadership

Abusive Expectations

The habit of abusing an employee and then asking the employee for assistance.

Healthy and Normal Function

Leaders treat all employees with respect and dignity. They praise subordinates in public and criticize in private, and have the common sense and decency to recognize that if you abuse an employee in public, they might not be so interested in saving the day for you later on.

Causes of Dysfunction

For the abuser:

- a feeling of superiority and general lack of concern for others
- willingness to create scapegoats
- recognition and exploitation of the fact that people have short memories and will likely forget boorish behavior over time

For the abused:

- a false need to regain one's reputation after the abuse
- the vulnerability of needing to keep one's job, resulting in the willingness to accept abuse
- a desperate need for validation, even twisted validation

Risk to the Organization

This type of behavior, if not satisfactorily addressed, becomes part of the corporate culture. When that occurs, the most confident employees will seek employment elsewhere and vocalize their concerns, severely damaging the reputation of the company.

Symptoms and Signs

- berating a subordinate in public and then asking for his or her help in private
- inspiring anger, frustration, and fear among staff members
- conflating supervision with indentured servitude
- maligning the best employees to keep them submissive
- hording the recognition for all successes

Diagnostic Analysis

- Is the behavior consistently displayed at public meetings?
- Does the individual use exploitation as a primary means of relating to others?
- Is there an apparent lack of concern for the harmful impact of self-interest-based actions on others?
- Do quality staff members leaving the organization verify the inappropriate behavior?

Progression and Impact

The progression of this disease is unique. The initial berating causes great concern among staff because it is unwarranted and done in a public setting. Then, in truly bizarre fashion, the same person who was publicly maligned is shortly thereafter given a critical project—or is encouraged to leave the organization but asked to stay on and assist with the transition. Strangely, more often than not, the employee obliges.

The first time this occurs, observers are dumbfounded. It seems unbelievable that management could treat someone this poorly and then follow it up with a request for assistance. But after repeated instances, this approach ceases to be an anomaly. It's like the strange uncle in the family—you don't know why he behaves the way he does, but he's family, so you endure it.

One explanation is that management promises maligned employees that the beatings will stop if they just announce they're leaving. Another explanation is that the employee has not yet secured other employment and is, therefore, willing to endure the abuse to gain a paycheck. Another is a misguided need to save face. After being maligned, some employees feel a sense of vindication if they are asked to stay and help out with the transition.

After seeing this behavior play out several times, the organization begins to accept it as a part of its culture. This is disappointing and reminiscent of an abused spouse staying because there is no place to go. Employees who stay with the organization acquiesce because they don't believe it will happen to them, or they are willing to be abused and play ball. This does not lay a solid foundation for attracting and retaining the best and brightest who can ensure an efficient and effective organization. Indeed, quite the opposite. This abusive behavior breeds a hapless, frightened, uncreative, and risk-adverse organization.

Prognosis

This disease can be abated only if the board of directors puts a stop to it. If not, then over the long term, the organization will develop a permanent, unsightly disability, limiting prospective employee suitors.

Treatment or Cure

Stopping the progress of the disease will involve one or more of the following:
- a majority of board members who are willing to quash the behavior
- an employee or two willing to calmly and articulately call management out when this type of behavior occurs
- ascertain the reason(s) for the unprofessional behavior and make any necessary adjustments
- negative media attention
- a lawsuit or two

Case Study

The Big Swallow

A health-care oversight function was created by elected officials to monitor and provide information regarding the proper care of indigent clients. From the outset, the function suffered from an inadequate definition of roles and responsibilities, as well as an inadequate understanding of the operational mandates of providing health-care services.

Rachel was manager of the oversight function. Over a five-year period, she was intermittently blamed by a minority of board members for the perceived ineffectiveness of the function; health-care officials, on the other hand, were pleased with her efforts. The board minority felt that Rachel should not be physically located at the health department, was too close to health-department officials to objectively monitor their activities, and provided insufficient updates to the board on important health issues.

Over time, the swing vote on the board flipped, resulting in a majority now calling for the dissolution of the department and the dismissal of Rachel. The swing voter based his dubious motive on not having been kept in the loop on the department's oversight activities; the real reason, however, appeared to be that the board member wanted control over the function to use for his personal ambitions at a later time.

Rachel was caught in a no-win situation. She was expected to satisfy both health care officials and the monitoring demands of elected officials; comply with confidentiality requirements while handing over all information to the elected officials; and navigate a minefield of political aspirations.

In order to facilitate the removal of Rachel, numerous questionable accusations were made. Eventually, this approach was criticized, and health care experts were asked to weigh in on the decision. The end result was that the organizational model for providing oversight was changed from a one-person manager to a multi-member panel.

During the interim period until the implementation of the new plan, one of the outside experts was asked to run the department on a part-time basis until the panel could be formed. Ironically, the outside expert retained Rachel to continue working for several months to keep the organization afloat. Apparently, the board had no problem maligning Rachel and then asking her to stay on for the transition. Surprisingly, she agreed to stay and serve in this capacity.

Lack of Shame

The inability or diminished capacity of a manager/executive ("the one") to feel embarrassment, disgrace, or ignominy for unscrupulous actions taken against others.

Healthy and Normal Function

Leaders and employees respect themselves and others, and they understand their joint responsibility for effectively and efficiently carrying out the mission and goals of the organization.

Causes of Dysfunction

- a consuming desire to maximize personal wealth, fame, or power
- antisocial personality disorder
- an inability to recognize when personal actions cause pain to others
- an outlook of work as a game with only winners and losers
- a feeling of entitlement based upon his or her position in the organization

Risk to the Organization

The risk to the organization is severe and potentially long-term. The narcissistic nature of this disease will make reasoning with the affected individual difficult, ensuring the continued disfigurement of the organization while "the one" bends the rules to meet his or her desires. If the disease is accompanied by a mediocre skill set, an organizational time bomb is ticking.

Symptoms and Signs

- feeling no embarrassment or shame, no matter how extreme the behavior
- refusing to apologize
- getting personal needs met before any other work can be done
- believing that no punishment is too severe for those who let "the one" down

Diagnostic Analysis

- Has there been a revolving door of employees hired and fired, with few complaints filed even though conditions are horrendous because of the certain fear of retaliation?
- Are staff members consistently and publicly belittled?

- Have employees grown accustomed to quick, explosive episodes of anger when "the one" does not get his or her way?
- Does "the one" derive his or her self-esteem from personal gain, power, or pleasure?
- Is there an apparent lack concern for the feelings, needs, or pain of others, and no remorse after hurting or mistreating others?
- Is exploitation "the one's" primary means of dealing with others?

Progression and Impact

Lack of shame is more often than not introduced into the organization by the board of directors, who in some cases embody this same disorder. When it becomes *the* most important task of the organization to meet the needs of its leaders, the concept of servant-leadership is transposed and disfigured, and those at the top are empowered to demand and expect adulation rather than provide a return on investment. Once this happens, leaders falsely believe that none of their behaviors are inappropriate or unseemly. This unbridled entitlement paves the way for abuse. The leader's wishes become the employees' commands. There simply is no shame in demanding or belittling those one believes exist to serve oneself.

Prognosis

This disease may be eventually fatal to an organization, although the length of time until potential expiration depends on the skill set of quality leaders and employees who courageously step in to mitigate the collapse.

Treatment or Cure

- Ensure a majority of board members whose first priority is to serve the company, as opposed to the company existing to serve its leaders.
- Hire a CEO whose primary mission is the efficient and effective operation of the organization, and who is expected to challenge and address any board member who goes beyond appropriate boundaries.
- Utilize selection tools during the interview process to identify and weed out anyone who demonstrates this type of personality disorder.
- Have a robust compliance/ethics function that is able to identify, expose, and appropriately address serious behavioral issues.

Case Study

What's Yours Is Mine

John was an unqualified candidate who was nonetheless hired as a department head. John's first year was riddled with poor choices based on loyalty and patronage, the false belief that he was chosen because of solid leadership and personal-relations skills, and a resulting sense of entitlement because of his status as a department head. The new inner circle was predictably unable to command respect with their lack of executive skills or accomplishments, so they ruled by fear.

The decisions of these executives could not be questioned, as it would expose the inner circle's lack of depth and ability for critical thinking. The circle used pat phrases to dissuade and shut down debate, such as, "Well, I guess we just have a different perspective." Meetings on important issues were closed to subject-matter experts because predetermined decisions had already been made based on political considerations. Those who, for the good of the organization, brought up important operational and ethical concerns were moved to other parts of the organization or had pay raises withheld.

Even though these managers were transferred, it was periodically necessary to reach out and utilize their services when critical issues arose that could not be solved politically. One such "critical" need was ensuring that John received a pay raise after his first year on the job. It was highly important to John and the inner circle to create the perception that the first year was a success. So John asked his best and brightest to review and edit a document that he prepared to showcase the year's accomplishments. In essence, John asked the talented employees he had recently tossed aside to help him write his performance evaluation.

Not surprisingly, the most important accomplishments and edits to the performance evaluation were achieved by those outside the inner circle. In a shameful display, John ultimately received a pay increase based on the accomplishments of those he would not give a pay raise to for actually doing the work.

The Aphrodisiac of Leadership

The use of a position of power and influence to predatorily seek out or accept sexual favors from employees.

Healthy and Normal Function

Employees are promoted based on merit, including emotional intelligence and character. Supervisors maintain healthy relationships with staff members and avoid compromising activities. Supervisors are dedicated to the needs and success of the organization above their own needs and ambitions.

Causes of Dysfunction

- view of leadership as a way to get what one wants, rather than to serve the organization
- desire for control over the economic rewards of the workplace
- seeing employees as a tool or commodity rather than a person
- desire to demonstrate raw power
- people in positions of leadership who do not demonstrate appropriate emotional intelligence or have significant character flaws

Risk to the Organization

The risk to the organization of this disorder is off the charts. Sexual-control cases usually result in termination and many times can reach the level of a criminal offense, depending upon the predatory nature and/or the unwillingness of the participants. Either way, if the organization makes the mistake of promoting an abusive individual to a position of power, let the lawsuits fly, take out your pocketbook, and buy as much disinfectant as you can—the organization will need it over the long term.

There will be many combinations, permutations, twists, and turns in the complaints from those impacted and those trying to hop on the gravy train. It will become a dizzying and draining experience for those assigned to clean up the mess. Try saying no to even frivolous claims that are related to the actions of a substantiated sexual predator.

Symptoms and Signs

- a pattern regarding the type of victim pursued and the methodology of the pursuit
- regular long periods away from his or her desk in the middle of the day
- hushed conversations in the stairwell or other out-of-the-way locations
- lunch with a number of employees of the opposite sex
- consistent comments about how attractive certain staff members look
- overly familiar and abnormal direct access to an executive not in his or her chain of command

Diagnostic Analysis

- What do victims or the friends of those who regularly have lunch or coffee with the predator have to say about these encounters?
- Is there evidence of impropriety in company-owned phone records and e-mails?
- When surreptitiously engaged in casual conversation, does the predator brag about his or her exploits?
- What is the predator's reaction to the suggestion that one of his or her victims may be transferred to another work location?
- Have formal complaints been filed against the predator?
- If surveillance video cameras have been installed, what do they show?

Progression and Impact

This disease obviously involves a severe character flaw in the predator. Sometimes the predator does not overtly demonstrate this type of behavior before coming into a position of power, as the opportunities are more limited at lower levels. If there is any indication that someone spends too much time in flirtatious behavior rather than working, it would behoove the organization to proceed slowly in promoting this individual.

This is particularly relevant if the predator has connections with the power brokers of the organization and is using those relationships to rise through the ranks. If the predator has successfully disguised this proclivity and has the backing of the power elite, it is likely that he or she feels able to get away with anything. This combination completes the sexual fire triangle (character defect, opportunity, connections) and makes the nightmare possible.

It is not uncommon for the predator to have a tried and true methodology. For instance, the predator may have certain physical and mental specifications for a victim—for example, a certain race, age range, physical attribute, aspiration of moving up in the organization, or confidence level. The predator may also utilize a consistent and progressive methodology for the chase: a friendly introduction to attractive newcomers, skillfully letting them know his or her position in the organization; an invitation to coffee with others during the day; an invitation to lunch alone to talk about work projects and work aspirations; periodic phone calls during the day to see how the victim is doing; an invitation to dinner immediately following work to discuss work issues, ostensibly because the predator couldn't fit it in during the day; the carefully crafted introduction of sex jokes to gauge the victim's receptiveness; and so on. Part of the perpetrator's methodology may also be like a typical sales strategy: the more calls one makes, the more chances for success. It is not uncommon for someone with this disorder to have many hooks in the water at varying depths with varying baits.

If this situation comes to an awful fruition and multiple complaints are filed, the reputation of the organization will take a substantial hit that takes years to overcome. It is the perfect news story: sex, power, abuse. It will be the sexual equivalent of a massive oil spill. Remediation activities will take years to complete, public opinion will have to be salvaged over time, lawsuits and potential criminal actions will be litigated, high-level executives will be fired and new leaders hired, promotions may be extorted to drop complaints, and the costs associated with all of this will be immense.

Prognosis

Depending upon the organizational level of the predator and how many victims there are, there is no bleaker prospect for an organization or the employees impacted. The organization will be apologizing and paying out for years to come.

Treatment or Cure

- Focus on early identification and mentoring of up-and-coming managers who appear to have a sexual sweet tooth. Monitor them closely. If there is no indication of a diminishment of the proclivity, do not promote this individual ever, for any reason.
- During mandated sexual-harassment training, identify management expectations and go through the penalties involved and the damage that may be caused to the organization.
- Identify situations where the elements of the sexual fire triangle come together.
- Take swift and severe action against any employee who uses a position of authority to take advantage of others.

Case Study

Sexploitation

Before Ricardo's rise in the organization, he was a politically connected up-and-comer with several highly placed friends in positions of authority. Ricardo was married and had children. During his rise, Ricardo had a habit of frequently mingling with members of the opposite sex. Intermittently, friends would caution him to be careful about perceptions and to refrain from doing anything that would hurt his marriage or chances for advancement. Ricardo would always smile, agree, and say he would be more careful.

Eventually, Ricardo was promoted to an executive position. In this new role, Ricardo accelerated his activities with young women in the organization who were looking to advance. Using his new position of authority, Ricardo began casting a wide net of casual meetings for coffee and lunch to discuss work projects, and then eventually dinner right after work to catch up on the day's activities and discuss the female's work aspirations. Many of these encounters developed into sexual relationships.

Over time, these relationships changed, and many women wanted to discontinue them. However, Ricardo used his power and high-level contacts as leverage to persuade some of the women to continue the relationship. Eventually, many relationships became strained and may have even involved the use of force. There were stories of sex in the office, not allowing women to leave his office, or threatening their careers.

Eventually, complaints were filed and investigated. At their conclusion, the case was turned over to local law enforcement, and Ricardo was charged with multiple felonies. The news of the event, the pretrial period, and Ricardo's ultimate plea of guilty to felony and misdemeanor charges raged on the front pages of the media for several years, casting an immensely negative PR light on the organization. Ricardo is now serving a jail sentence.

Chapter 3

Behavioral Deficiencies: Fear Based

Fight or Flight

- Abdication to the Malicious Minority
- Fear of Conflict
- Control Freak
- Failure to Secure Executive Buy-In
- Hiding Information
- Imposter Complex
- Lack of Courage
- Postponing the Delivery of Bad News
- Purging the Competition
- Speaking without Saying Anything

Abdication to the Malicious Minority

The ceding of control to the unmerited minority position of the nastiest SOB in the room.

Healthy and Normal Function

Each leader states his or her position in a calm and rational manner based on facts, and the best argument carries the day. The primary objective is to make the best decision for the organization—aligned with its mission and goals—without regard to personal gain or loss. The majority believes that making concessions on principle is not an option.

Causes of Dysfunction

- not worth the energy to take on the SOB
- winning the battle not worth losing the SOB's vote or support at a later time on a more important issue
- SOB makes life miserable for those who disagree
- anticipation of having the favor returned

Risk to the Organization

Allowing the minority's unmerited opinion to rule on an issue brings significant risk to an organization. Typically, this situation becomes particularly acute when the minority is allowed to block a good idea, push through a bad one, or wrongly punish an ethical person who gets in its way. The obvious problem is that on many important issues, doing the right thing for the right reason is not implemented because the majority chooses not to take a stand against the SOB.

As a result, the bully gets rewarded, notes the behaviors that succeeded, and repeats them in the future. This abdication of responsibility precludes democratic governing by allowing a deeply flawed or even malicious person to control an entire body. If this method enjoys continued success, word quickly gets out that it is not safe to have a different viewpoint from that of the SOB, and the implementation of minority positions is institutionalized.

Symptoms and Signs

- skilled, ethical people passed over for promotion in favor of more brittle and persuadable employees
- extreme sensitivity to criticism and subsequent retaliation by SOB if things don't go his or her way
- opposition to good projects if they are proposed by those who sometimes disagree with the SOB
- those in favor of the majority position dropping their heads and mumbling when asked why they voted against their conscience
- well-intentioned employees changing their behaviors, recommendations, and positions to avoid negative repercussions from the SOB
- difficulty in getting a quorum for doing the right thing

Diagnostic Analysis

- Does the SOB have the perception that people are either totally for or totally against them?
- Do solidly supported proposals for good projects lose the day after the malicious minority threatens other board members?
- Have there been media hit pieces by the SOB against those who disagree with the minority position?
- Are employees increasingly reluctant to take personal risks and sensitive to criticism and rejection?

Progression and Impact

This disease can be neutralized if dealt with quickly and firmly at its onset. Just like a bully on the playground, the metaphorical punch in the nose usually does the trick. If not addressed, this disease will spread rather quickly and have sustainability ramifications for the organization.

Once the SOB knows how to win, he or she will relentlessly pursue this strategy of volume and vitriol. After all, it is easier to bully an individual than to defend a bad idea. The SOB must win every confrontation. It's just like feeding table food to one's pet—the pet will shortly demand caviar by barking or whining incessantly. Soon, the human is the one who is trained, giving in more quickly in each situation. Reversing this ingrained behavior will require drastic and sustained effort.

The SOB will fight tooth and nail not to relinquish power, and he or she will threaten others in innumerable ways if they do not acquiesce. The SOB's winning formula is to increase the other person's suffering to get his or her own way. At a certain point, submission by the SOB may not be possible, and the ensuing winner-take-all battle will be staged in full view of the entire organization. Either the cult or the culture will prevail.

Prognosis

If the SOB's behavior is not addressed, the organization will, for all practical purposes, be run by this one individual. Those with character will retreat, and those without it will be assimilated.

Treatment or Cure

The cure is easily stated but hard for many people to administer: in an unemotional manner, firmly disagree with the SOB, calling him or her out with facts and evidence that demonstrate the unprofessional nature of this individual's behavior to the group, and its negative impact on the business. Be prepared to face immediate spurious accusations, both internally and publicly. If treatment is delayed, more aggressive and unrelenting efforts must be administered to eradicate the disease. To win, you must be willing to force an intervention. You cannot give in at any cost, or you will be owned by the SOB.

Case Study

Nero's Zeros and Ones

A private organization received vendor proposals for the provision of a mission-critical, multimillion-dollar IT service contract over several years. The low-bid proposal was submitted by a company with questionable experience providing the service. One member of the board of directors, Bill, was close to the lobbyist for the low-bid vendor, and he was also looking to be placed on the vendor's board of directors. Bill aggressively pushed for the low-bid vendor to get the contract, making a number of business threats if he didn't get his way. Because of Bill's pressure, the questionable vendor's proposal was chosen by a slight majority of board members.

Not surprisingly, the chosen vendor could not adequately perform the service, with severe operational consequences to the organization and the waste of millions of dollars of stockholder money. By this time, Bill had left the organization and moved on to greener pastures. The organization was left holding the bag, and it spent significant time and additional millions of dollars trying to extricate itself from the contract.

Fear of Conflict

A reluctance or unwillingness to address issues that might result in disagreements with employees.

Healthy and Normal Function

It is important to point out that nobody should really *like* conflict. Don't pick supervisors who enjoy being in the middle of controversy. Organizations should want managers who would prefer that there not be conflict and will work to avoid it, but are also ready, willing, and able to handle it when and if necessary.

Causes of Dysfunction

- fear of ongoing ill feelings with staff
- fear of grievances or lawsuits
- awareness of the excessive time it takes to get rid of a problem employee, and the boss's lack of support if the process becomes difficult
- insufficient interpersonal or performance management skills
- a performance record that makes it difficult to call out another employee

Risk to the Organization

The risk to the organization of avoiding conflict is that the inmates will rule the asylum. Every supervisor–subordinate relationship has some degree of conflict. If a supervisor is not willing to supervise, company rules and those in authority will eventually be ignored.

Symptoms and Signs

- procrastination or failure to address subordinate performance issues
- supervisor or employee primarily staying in his or her office
- employees pushing the envelope by doing such things as coming into work late, leaving early, or only working on projects they want to
- problems that fester and become bigger issues, followed by blowups from a lack of resolution

Diagnostic Analysis

- Do a vast majority of performance evaluations fail to identify any areas for employee improvement?
- Who appears to be running the organization: the supervisor or the employees?
- What do employees have to say when asked about their boss?
- What consequences are meted out for in-your-face behavior by subordinates?
- Does hypersensitivity to criticism result in a reluctance to take risks?
- Does the supervisor seem uncomfortable in social settings and insecure about his or her skill sets?

Progression and Impact

Some people don't mind being in charge or having to work with others to solve tough problems. Some supervisors just like people, like the challenge, and enjoy debating in general. Maybe they just enjoy telling other people what to do and proving themselves right. Others, however, are deathly afraid of disagreement and standing their ground. They will do anything to avoid unpleasantness. Sometimes this is related to personality, sometimes to a confidence issue, and sometimes to a preference for staying underground and not making any waves.

This disease can be contained if it is limited to only a few supervisors. However, if the supervisory ranks are sprinkled with those who prefer to avoid conflict, the organization will suffer. Issues will go unresolved, supervision will be only a suggestion, and those with the strongest and perhaps most bullying personalities will have a distinct advantage. Employees will decide which company rules they want to follow and which they don't.

As a result, projects and services will not be delivered on time. This condition will be extremely difficult to fix, as those in supervision who were hired to solve problems *are* the problem. The CEO will have to evaluate the competence levels of his or her supervisors and make necessary changes. Until this situation is resolved, the company will be like the Wild West.

Prognosis

If addressed in a reasonable time frame, this condition is curable and may turn out to be a healthy challenge for the organization to face and conquer. If not, the disease will slowly spread. A company that never fully addresses its lack of backbone will eventually go out of business.

Treatment or Cure

- Don't hire people for supervisory positions who show absolutely no aptitude or desire for it.
- Provide training and mentoring to help supervisors deal with conflict and conduct crucial conversations.
- Demand accurate performance reviews.
- Insist that supervisors deal with conflict as it arises. Stand up or stand down—no riding the fence.

Case Study

The Deer Hunter

An investigation was conducted concerning an employee who allegedly shot a deer while at work on a construction site in an urban environment. During initial questioning, the site supervisor claimed to be unaware of the incident. When the employee was questioned, he eventually admitted shooting the deer but insisted he had done nothing wrong.

The employee felt justified because it was hunting season, he had a license, and the deer was in a location away from workers. The only argument that seemed to resonate with the worker was that he had shot the deer on company time when he should have been working. When the investigator asked how the employee managed to get the deer loaded into his truck, the employee casually responded that his supervisor helped him. When questioned further, the employee stated that the supervisor drove him to the location, was present while the deer was shot, and helped him first load the deer into the supervisor's truck and then transfer it to the employee's truck.

When the supervisor was asked why he participated in this event, he stated with embarrassment that it seemed like a fun thing to do, and he didn't want to spoil an employee's fun. As a result, the employee's discipline was reduced to a reprimand and the supervisor was suspended for failing to perform his supervisory duty.

Control Freak

An individual who exerts debilitating, micromanaging control over subordinates and their assignments, precluding them from learning and becoming proficient at their tasks.

Healthy and Normal Function

Employees are adequately trained and provided with sensible supervisory control and oversight to allow for the learning of tasks while ensuring that work is done correctly. The company accepts that some failures can lead to productive learning sessions and remains open to those opportunities. Supervisors and employees are open to learning better ways of doing things.

Causes of Dysfunction

- fear of failure
- feeling of intense pressure to succeed
- belief that no one can do it better
- concern over time and resource constraints, to the point that the supervisor must become involved in the employees' efforts

Risk to the Organization

The risks to the organization include stunting the growth of the next generation of leaders, reducing the productivity of the unit because the Control Freak has to be involved in all projects, and preventing new ideas from being tried.

Symptoms and Signs

- supervisor constantly hovering over subordinates
- few opportunities available to try new solutions
- sense of exasperation by employees over having their work redone
- general worker malaise and lack of ownership of projects
- meetings, meetings, and more meetings
- lack of vacation time taken by the supervisor
- increased time necessary to complete tasks because of stifling oversight

Diagnostic Analysis

- Can staff members provide examples of excessive oversight?
- Is permission required for finalizing all decisions?
- Is the supervisor in a constant state of anxiety?
- Is the supervisor's self-esteem based entirely on work?
- Does the supervisor believe that there is only one right way to do things and insist on perfection in all projects?
- Does the supervisor recognize futile situations and know when to pull the plug?

Progression and Impact

Fortunately, this disorder is generally limited because it unnecessarily increases work and stress levels. However, if it is found at the top of the organization, it can quickly spread many levels down. Leaders who need to know every detail of what direct reports are doing inspire the same level of control all the way down the chain of command. This condition can have significant negative consequences for the organization, including the following:

- Supervisors are so busy checking on subordinates that they have no time to do their own work.
- Employees never learn how to complete a task from beginning to end under their own steam—or have the opportunity to learn from their mistakes.
- The organization becomes stale and lacks creativity because work can only be done the Control Freak's way.
- Employees don't feel validated or trusted.
- Employees eventually do a marginal job because they know the Control Freak will jump in and "fix" whatever they miss.

Prognosis

If this disorder has a limited presence, it can be identified and addressed rather quickly with appropriate mentoring and performance management. However, if it is not addressed or is contracted by someone at the top of the organization, it becomes far more difficult to manage. It may take a worker uprising to get the attention of management to bring things back into balance.

Treatment or Cure

- Attempt to ascertain the reason(s) for the Control Freak's behavior, and if company executives or subordinates have contributed to the problem.
- Have a frank conversation with affected individuals, pointing out the negative consequences of this management style. For difficult cases, consider discussing how the supervisor would feel if this management style were utilized on them.
- Ensure that Control Freaks take sufficient vacation time and don't call in.
- Give the Control Freak a special project with the caveat that he or she has to complete it personally so he or she doesn't have time to overcontrol subordinates.

Case Study

Gridlock

Lydia was a supervisor who wanted to be informed about every important issue that came up within her sphere of influence. The problem was that she never satisfactorily defined "important." As a result, everyone had to learn the hard way what Lydia felt was important, which unfortunately changed on a weekly basis. "The hard way" meant verbal berating in public and phone calls at all hours of the day and night.

Lydia was a micromanager who figured that if she was still awake, her subordinates should be as well, making their supervisor look good on a 24-7 basis. Eventually, her subordinates decided in an abundance of caution that everything should be considered important. That meant that everyone was trying to communicate with Lydia on a nonstop basis. Very soon, her calendar, e-mail inbox, and voice mail box were full, and there was, at times, no way to reach her with truly important information.

Micromanagement led to gridlock and frustration for both Lydia and her subordinates. As expected, Lydia lost a lot of talented employees who self-selected out of the menagerie.

Failure to Secure Executive Buy-In

The assignment of an extensive level of company resources to a project prior to receiving authorization from executives.

Healthy and Normal Function

Projects are proposed and reviewed through the normal chain of command, using appropriate criteria. If a project is not approved and there is a sufficient negative reaction, a meeting is called to further discuss the merits of the project. There is a willingness to move the project higher up the chain of command if it is that important to the workers at the ground floor. Once a decision has been made, all must live with it. Anyone who cannot should contemplate leaving the organization rather than being insubordinate.

Causes of Dysfunction

- certainty that company leaders are going to say yes to the project, so there's no need to wait around for approval before getting started
- belief that the way to push through a controversial project is to do so under the radar
- belief that it is better to ask for forgiveness than permission
- lack of confidence in the decisions and choices of leadership

Risk to the Organization

The risk to the organization is that significant time and money will be invested in a project that may not have the support of company leadership and does not align with the company's mission, goals, or values.

Symptoms and Signs

- limited discussion about a particular project
- projects purposely left off the status report
- monies quietly moved around to secure project funding
- strong staff support for a project but uncertainty from management

Diagnostic Analysis

- Are there rumors of unauthorized projects being performed?
- Are there any vague project expenditures on status reports?
- Are executives surprised to hear about a particular project?
- Is there a history of other projects moved forward prior to receiving appropriate authorization? Have there been any consequences for this practice?
- Is there a history of managers asking for forgiveness rather than permission?

Progression and Impact

Sometimes, this disorder occurs as an impromptu reaction to seeing something that needs to be done. Middle management may commit staff and dollars without thinking to ask permission because it never occurs to them that anyone would disagree with the project. In such cases, it is hoped that at some point early in the process, staff thinks to inform upper management—or management, during the course of field visits, notices the start of the new project.

On the other hand, sometimes this situation occurs because the proposed project has been met with a degree of resistance and staff is insistent that it be accomplished. The progression and impact of this situation is related to how clandestine the supporters of the project are willing to be. In its most benign form, those who seek the completion of the project are willing to quietly push it forward, hoping that they can persuade upper management of its merits after it has already begun. In more questionable practices, employees move the project forward at full speed in the hope that it will be too late to turn back once executives realize how far along they are. Even rarer are the times when project supporters hope to complete a small project quietly and never discuss it, hoping that it flies under the radar.

It is important that project supporters understand the level of risk in moving an unauthorized project forward. The consequences may be just a slap on the wrist and a promise never to repeat something like this, or someone may get fired. Those committing to the project must be willing to accept the consequences of their choices.

Prognosis

The prognosis is typically good for a rare occurrence with minimal impact. However, direct insubordination and misdirection of company resources for an unauthorized project must be addressed. If an individual is willing to take the risk, he or she had better hope the project is a critical success.

Treatment or Cure

There is no specific treatment or cure for this disease. One either takes the risk and survives or does not. If you commit to this path, you must be willing to accept the consequences.

Case Study

Grant Gamble

Every year in a particular organization, grant monies became available for certain projects. In one instance, Marta felt that the company had an excellent opportunity to receive a public service grant for an important project her staff wanted to pursue. It was unclear, however, if applying for the grant would receive the majority support of the board of directors because of questionable political and personal concerns of some board members. Because line staff strongly believed in the project, Marta chose not to risk asking for permission to apply for the grant. So she applied for the funds without properly notifying the board.

The grant proposal was approved, but unbeknownst to Marta and her staff, the grantor publicized all grant recipients and their proposed projects. When some of the board members learned of the award, they were furious that the company policy of getting the board's prior authorization had not been followed. Marta's department head disciplined her for failing to secure authorization for the project. In addition, the department received increased scrutiny for over a year, adding to implementation time frames.

In an interesting footnote, the project was a critical success in the community, for which all the board members took credit.

Hiding Information

The deliberate withholding of important need-to-know information from others in the organization.

Healthy and Normal Function

Information should be freely shared with all those who have a need to know so that the best decisions can be reached and the corresponding actions implemented. Employees should not be rewarded for withholding information. Promotions should be based on legitimate skill sets and abilities, not on how devious someone can be. While an occasional degree of game-playing may occur, organizational health is always more important than individual wealth.

Causes of Dysfunction

- desire to secure and maintain organizational power and control
- attempt to conceal illegitimate activities or mistakes
- lack of trust in others
- desire to conceal management weaknesses
- opportunity to possess damaging information against others

Risk to the Organization

There are innumerable risks to an organization in allowing an employee to conceal information from colleagues. Besides the basic fact that work activities can't be efficiently or effectively accomplished, it encourages others to hid information as well, evaporating trust throughout the organization. Inefficiency, ineffectiveness, and distrust combine to flatline the company.

Symptoms and Signs

- locked files without titles
- information used for personal rather than organizational gain
- uneasiness and a lack of trust around certain people
- crucial information discovered after the fact
- caginess and cryptic responses to important questions

Diagnostic Analysis

- Does research and investigation—examining paper and computer files—reveal buried information?
- In interviews, do affected employees tell stories of hiding information or seeing others do so?
- Has previously unreleased information been revealed at opportune times to ensure the highest negative impact?
- Are there individuals who frequently use questionable tactics to achieve their own ends while showing little genuine interest in others' success and an overbearing interest in their own?
- Are positive outcomes overturned as a result of hiding information?

Progression and Impact

Hiding information from those who need it for the legitimate operation of the organization is self-defeating. It's like having only two numbers to one's combination lock. *Click, click, cluck.* In today's world, information is power and necessary to keep pace with the competition.

Withholding of necessary information usually comes from a negative motivation for personal gain at the expense of the company, and it always negatively impacts people. Decisions get made with the wrong information and scarce resources are wasted; people's reputations are maligned; positive outcomes are overturned; the wrong people get promoted; and distrust spreads throughout the organization.

This type of behavior is typically associated with attempting to increase one's organizational power or hide questionable actions. If it is not monitored and addressed, others will copy the behavior to secure a competitive advantage or retain the status quo. Everybody has to have dirt to nullify each other's dirt. It's like the self-defeating actions of the CIA and FBI withholding information from each other.

Prognosis

There is a natural limit to the amount of information-hoarding that can go on. If everybody withholds information, there is no reason to come to work. In addition, as in baking, withholding even a little bit of the right ingredient can make the cake go flat.

Treatment or Cure

- Have definitive roles and responsibilities for each major function/player so that it is clear what kinds of information each group/person is entitled to.
- The CEO and/or board of directors must monitor this type of behavior, isolate it, and discontinue its practice.
- Don't hire or retain people who feel the need to get ahead based on subversive activities.

Case Study

Consequential Cover-Up

Clarence, a newly promoted company executive, used his position of power to have sex with multiple young, career-motivated females. After a complaint was filed, the investigation was manipulated by having it assigned to one of Clarence's subordinates—who, of course, found the charges to be unsubstantiated.

After additional complaints were filed in multiple venues, a legitimate investigation was farmed out to a private investigator. After the investigation was complete, a report was sent to the COO that substantiated several charges, including possible criminal behavior. Rather than discuss the significance of the report with the board, fire the executive, and refer the case to law enforcement, involved C-suite personnel concealed the report and, behind the scenes, quietly asked Clarence to leave the organization with a severance package.

The existence of the report was eventually uncovered by an auditor, and was then sent by legal counsel to law enforcement. Clarence was ultimately charged with several felonies. The initial withholding and inadequate addressing of this information resulted in several severe consequences, including the following:

- delayed justice to the victims
- reputation damage because of media reporting of all the salacious details of power, sex, and politics
- a conspiracy investigation for concealing of information pertaining to a crime
- significant damage to employee morale and trust in their employer
- lawsuits
- costly and time-consuming activities to ensure and overtly prove that the organization was addressing the issue, albeit after the fact

Imposter Complex

The fear that people will find out that one is not sufficiently qualified for one's position in the organization.

Healthy and Normal Function

Those promoted to any job within the organization must possess the requisite skills, experience, and education. Periodic appraisals are conducted on each manager and executive to verify performance and to ensure the possession of necessary skills and abilities. Malicious imposters are uncloaked and disappear as soon as they are discovered; salvageable imposters are counseled and trained to improve their deficiencies.

Causes of Dysfunction

- insufficient experience, education, or other requisite skills to competently perform the duties of his or her position
- receiving an undeserved promotion
- fear of being exposed, balanced against the belief that he or she might be able to fool most of the people most of the time
- recognition that there are other imposters at large in the organization
- determination to get ahead in the only way possible

Risk to the Organization

The risk to the organization is that the imposter's efforts in covering up inadequacies takes time away from essential duties and typically results in bad decisions made from a lack of experience.

Symptoms and Signs

- appearing to be at a loss for knowing where to start on a new job
- avoiding discussion of work specifics
- sending other people to meetings in one's stead
- uncanny ability to identify other imposters
- having others write all of one's communications
- false portrayal of confidence to mask one's sense of inadequacy

- imposter's only work product is thinking big thoughts all day; little to no evidence of written analytical work completed
- trying to be out of the office by going to a lot of conferences
- avoiding direct participation in the work
- not staying too long in any one job

Diagnostic Analysis

- Do the individual's application and job-interview statements contain misleading information or misrepresentation of abilities?
- Is the individual sensitive to criticism or afraid of being exposed for a lack of adequate talent for his or her position?
- How does the individual respond when given real work to do or asked for examples of past written work product?
- Is the individual able to answer technical questions about specific organizational issues?
- Is the individual able to have meaningful conversations about critical work subjects?
- What do the individual's direct reports have to say about him or her?

Progression and Impact

The impact of this disease is largely dependent upon the number of imposters and their placement in the organizational food chain. If located near the top of the food chain, the imposter has an interesting dilemma: either hire fellow imposters so that no one can take his or her place, or hire people with real skills and abilities who can cover and make up for the imposter's deficiencies. Obviously, if the imposter chooses the former, the impact to the organization is far more disruptive.

To successfully cover up inadequacies, imposters must take drastic precautions. They must ensure that no one gets close enough to see behind the curtain. In order to do this, anyone who even appears to challenge their authority, the veracity of their claims, or the correctness of their decisions must be intensely berated in public so no one will ever again attempt it. In private, the imposter must go even further, threatening any challenger with discipline or termination for showing such indiscretion. On the reverse side, the imposter must lavishly praise and reward subordinates for producing results and not raising issues or asking probing questions. This Pavlovish technique will extinguish dissent and engrain the needed behaviors among the staff.

If subordinates know that their boss is an imposter, they are in a difficult situation, as they must cover up for his or her inadequacies. These subordinates will have to do their job as well as their leader's and be content that the leader will take all the credit. Covering up for someone takes an inordinate amount of time, as the big lie must be covered up with continuous small lies that require creativity and a good memory. All these efforts take away from making a profit and meeting the needs of the customer.

Having an imposter in charge also leads to poor resource and personnel decisions. While the imposter might try to defer these decisions to qualified subordinates, it is simply too difficult to remove the leader from all critical decisions, as some will inevitably come up in front of other people. Even worse, sometimes imposters believe their own hype and convince themselves that the good decisions made by subordinates were the result of their leadership. After all, if one can fool the masses, one just might be able to fool oneself as well.

Typically, this house of cards eventually crumbles, with severe embarrassment to the organization and a realization that significant resources have been wasted because of poor decisions and actions.

Prognosis

If the disease is quarantined to a few individuals in less significant positions, the organization can survive and regroup after some inevitable turnover. However, if the disease proliferates based on the imposter's hiring of other imposters, the company's reputation and bottom line will suffer extensively, and many good employees will be lost.

Treatment or Cure

- The board of directors must prohibit political appointments.
- Create a thorough and objective performance appraisal process.
- Develop and enforce a policy to prevent the gratuitous employment of relatives and friends.
- Give equal weight to IQ and EQ skills when making hiring decisions.
- Conduct recruitments with qualified interview-panel members.
- Implement periodic workforce surveys to gauge employee attitudes about the quality of their leaders.
- Provide training to improve deficiencies.

Case Study

"I'm Good Enough, I'm Smart Enough, and Doggone It, People Like Me!"[4]

Fred was promoted to the executive ranks because he had excellent technical skills. Unfortunately, he had atrocious interpersonal and EQ skills. While he could analyze and offer quality solutions to operational issues, he had absolutely no idea how to relate to another human being. The condition was so severe that it appeared that he didn't even know how to relate to himself. He clearly felt inadequate in any social interaction, and it appeared that he was not sure he belonged in a leadership position.

As much as this was painfully apparent to everyone, Fred wasted considerable time trying to hide his interpersonal inadequacies. He wrongly assumed that at any moment his personal inadequacies might be exposed. As such, Fred was careful never to allow anyone to get close to him or believe they were qualified enough to take his place. To achieve this, Fred scheduled periodic belittling sessions with all subordinates. In addition, when staff asked personal questions in an attempt to try to get to know him, Fred would either dodge the question or answer in such a way as to discourage additional questions.

Staff members dealing with Fred felt that everything was a competition that he had to win. Eventually, Fred decided to leave the organization because his behavior became more and more embarrassingly transparent. In a sad self-fulfilling prophecy, Fred's superiors could not stomach having personal dealings with him on any consistent basis.

[4] Al Franken, "Daily Affirmation with Stuart Smalley," *Saturday Night Live*, 1991, produced by Lorne Michaels.

Lack of Courage

Knowing the right thing to do but lacking the fortitude to do it.

Healthy and Normal Function

An organization values doing the right thing for the right reason, realizes that it is good for business, and seeks out and rewards those who responsibly demonstrate it in the workplace.

Causes of Dysfunction

- belief that doing the wrong thing is sometimes more lucrative
- concern that doing the right thing sometimes results in negative consequences—dismissal, no future promotional opportunities, or harassment
- unwanted confrontation from taking courageous action
- peer pressure to avoid making others feel guilty and/or insecure for their lack of courage
- sets future expectations for doing the right thing, thus limiting one's options

Risk to the Organization

The risk for the organization and employees under the supervision of those who lack courage is significant and can be emotionally wrenching. If an insufficient number of leaders stand up and call out clear injustices, employees will become profoundly disappointed with the organization and productivity will suffer, making it difficult to accomplish desired goals and objectives.

Symptoms and Signs

- taking great pains to stay under the radar
- reluctance to stand up for or lead any cause
- willingness to sell out others when necessary to avoid any personal pain or discomfort
- insistence, when asked to testify about something witnessed, that one didn't see anything, or doesn't have an opinion
- willingness to consistently make excuses for top leaders when they are wrong
- personal safety and well-being are of primary importance

Diagnostic Analysis

- Is the individual unwilling to go on the record for an offense he or she has witnessed?
- Does the individual ever deliver bad news up the chain of command?
- Has the individual ever accepted personal responsibility for a mistake?
- Has the individual turned down opportunities to lead a significant organizational project with large consequences for failure?
- Is the individual willing to allow others to suffer for something they didn't do?
- Has the individual thrown others under the bus if it advances his or her position in the organization?
- Has the individual ever challenged management on obvious bad ideas or proposed violations of company policy?

Progression and Impact

The progression of this disease depends on the number and level of persons in leadership who have chosen to contract it. If the disease is present at the top of the organization, the impact is immediate, pervasive, and crippling. Employees take their cue from the top. If leaders lack courage, others will be persuaded to adopt the same fearful and selfish approach. Indeed, making the boss look bad by demonstrating courage is generally not rewarded.

Those with courage will feel intermittently frustrated, maligned, and abused. Displaying courage to a timid boss is the equivalent of holding up a mirror that reflects sunlight into the boss's eyes. It is blinding and extremely uncomfortable. The boss cannot continue to look at the mirror without significant damage. The overwhelming reaction will be to break the mirror (you).

Another related aberration worth mentioning, because of its insidiousness, is punishing a courageous subordinate because he or she makes the boss's life difficult with the board of directors by doing the right thing. There will always be at least one board member who is willing to accomplish personal goals at the expense of the organization. Board members are in a position of power, free from removal absent considerable pushback, and their vote is always needed at some point in time. For this self-serving board member, anyone who stands in the way of accomplishing illegitimate pursuits becomes the enemy. If that enemy happens to be you, and you report to the head of the organization, expect both of your lives to be negatively impacted. Although your boss knows you are in the right, if he or she is subjected to a daily/weekly barrage of threats from a self-serving board member, it just becomes easier for the boss if you go away.

This outcome is particularly likely if you have a boss who lacks well-rounded experience or confidence and courage (supposedly prerequisites for a job at this level). Such bosses simply won't have the intestinal fortitude to directly confront and push back on the board member. In the end, in a great display of injustice, the employee will be punished for speaking up and the perpetrator will continue to pillage the organization. Obviously, this in turn creates fear among employees, limits passengers on the integrity train, and creates new (very) minimal qualifications for leadership positions. In fact, in this scenario, those at the top prefer a lack of courage.

Prognosis

This disease must be extracted from the organization's leaders or it will be terminal. If allowed to remain, it will result in a steady decline of those willing to demonstrate courage in the workplace and will have several damaging outcomes, including the following:

- inability to proactively address foreseeable calamities
- sacrifice of the best and brightest employees
- institutionalization of mediocrity in the workplace
- eventual transition from the unethical to the illegal

Treatment or Cure

- Evaluate your own and your subordinates' specific fears of taking courageous action and estimate the likelihood of those bad things actually happening. Discuss your own concerns with your superior or an executive coach. To help your employees overcome their fears, assign increasingly difficult projects, with an adviser to assist and serve as a temporary safety net.
- Create a safe environment where employees can express legitimate concerns without fear of reprisal.
- Insist that employees take on meaningful projects by themselves. Let them experience a limited amount of failure, measure the response, and then brief them on how to avoid future mistakes.
- Absolutely do not promote people with a demonstrated lack of courage into top positions; if they are already there, bump them back to the right level.
- Deal appropriately with any employees who stand by and allow another to be falsely accused, maligned, and wrongly found guilty if they know the truth to be different.

Case Study

Brinkmanship

Ted was the CFO for a public entity. Part of his responsibility was to cost out the financial impact of proposed collective bargaining agreements with labor unions. In one deal, a tentative agreement had been reached to substantially increase the retirement benefit for a particular bargaining unit. In essence, the proposal called for an approximate 50 percent increase in retirement pay and at the same time lowered the retirement age from sixty-two years of age to fifty-two. In addition, the enhanced benefit would be entirely retroactive. That meant that once the enhanced retirement benefit was approved, an employee already at age fifty-two could retire immediately and get the increased pay percentage applied to all their previous years of service. This enhanced benefit was being negotiated in several other public jurisdictions, which could have a negative impact on employee retention if not approved in Ted's organization.

Logically and intuitively, such an enhancement to a retirement formula would cost the public millions of dollars and substantially add to its unfunded pension liability. Yet, unbelievably, the agenda item calling for the approval of the new package by elected officials stated that there would be no increased costs associated with the enhancement. Not surprisingly, the tentative agreement came under intense scrutiny from the media. As a result, the public meeting for hearing the item was crammed full of ardent supporters and dissenters.

At the meeting, the elected officials appeared split over whether or not to approve the deal. In an effort to clarify costs, one elected official called the CFO up to the podium and in dramatic fashion asked, "I am asking you directly, as the CFO, whether or not there will be an increase in cost as a result of this proposal."

This was the moment the dissenters in the room were waiting for. Everyone knew the proposal had to cost taxpayers millions of dollars. Ted couldn't possibly avoid answering truthfully because of the unambiguity of the question. On the other side, the proponents had woven an elaborate "spin" on the issue and had spent all their political capital in lobbying the elected officials. The audience was utterly silent awaiting the CFO's answer.

The CFO hesitated for nearly five seconds, scanning the environment, gulping, and appearing to look deep within his soul. After a big breath in, the CFO stated the proposal would not generate additional costs. The proposal subsequently passed on a 3–2 vote.

Shortly thereafter, the CFO retired, unable to live with the damage to his credibility. Not long afterward, it became clear that the costs of these enhanced retirement packages given across the nation were so substantial that they crippled many public entities' general funds—and, in some cases, substantially contributed to the entities declaring bankruptcy.

Postponing the Delivery of Bad News

The determination to avoid or postpone the delivery of bad news to one's superiors.

Healthy and Normal Function

The organization encourages and trains its employees that it is in everyone's best interest to inform management as soon as possible of critical events that could damage the company. After a critical event occurs, those employees who followed the notification policy are praised, and the event becomes a learning experience.

Causes of Dysfunction

- fear of having to accept responsibility for the bad news
- desire to gain time to fix the situation, see if it goes away, see if anyone notices, construct a cover-up, or see if someone else can deliver the bad news
- belief that nothing is ever one's fault, or at least no one can prove that it is one's fault, so let someone else deliver the bad news

Risk to the Organization

As the saying goes, "Bad news never gets better with age." Avoiding or postponing the delivery of bad news delays potential action to mitigate the situation. One might get lucky, with the issue resolving itself with minimal impact—but if it doesn't, precious opportunities will have been lost to deal with the issue before it gets worse.

Symptoms and Signs

- repeated use of the word "wait" when anyone picks up the phone to deliver the bad news, followed by "let's think this through"
- avoidance of the boss
- everyone using the exact same phrases to describe the situation
- seeking someone who was not involved in the issue to deliver the bad news
- talking out loud to oneself to see how different scenarios sound
- increase in chatter and rumors about the situation
- missing of other work deadlines while trying to figure out a solution
- boxes being filled with personal belongings

Diagnostic Analysis

- When asking the most agitated person in the room what happened, what answer do you get?
- Is there an increase in "High Importance (!)" e-mails, and what do they say?
- Does the boss explode when he or she is finally notified?
- Have there been calls from regulatory agencies?
- Do employees exhibit habitual hypersensitivity to criticism or rejection?
- Is there a feeling of constant anxiety over negative situations and a projecting of worst-case scenarios?

Progression and Impact

The impact of this disease is heavily linked to the severity of the negative outcomes that result from postponing the delivery of bad news. For example, if one forgets to disclose that a coworker is on vacation, this would probably be chalked up as an oversight. However, if one forgets to disclose that one missed the deadline for a $20 million grant, that would be quite a different story.

If there are minimal or no negative outcomes from failure to promptly deliver bad news, this might weigh in as a mitigating factor in determining an appropriate response to the employee's inaction. However, one cannot rely on luck, and the organization cannot look past significant instances of non-notification. The risks are too great, and playing Russian roulette is not an option. Doing so would encourage additional instances of dodging responsibility and even more reckless behavior. The behavior must be extinguished when it occurs.

Prognosis

The prognosis is good if the instances in which this behavior occurs are related to minor events, or if the organizational response is severe enough to substantially discourage its repeated practice. However, the prognosis is bleak if this is the employee's modus operandi for negative events.

Treatment or Cure

- Make it standard operating procedure and active protocol to inform the chain of command within so many hours of certain kinds or levels of incidents occurring.
- Administer significant discipline to employees whose failure to disclose or postponement of disclosure results in significant consequences for the organization.
- Include this type of situation in the questions asked during the hiring process for employees.

Case Study

Illegiti-minimize

After two years as a department head within a large organization, Ivan decided that it was time to administer a workforce survey to ascertain the attitudes of employees toward the organization. Ivan was cautioned to expect that the results of the survey would probably not be that good and that employees would demand the results be distributed. Ivan chose to move forward.

The survey results were indeed atrocious, particularly in the areas of ethics, the direction the organization was heading, and employee rewards. Ivan was counseled to inform the CEO and board of directors of the survey results within a week and to follow up with a preliminary plan for addressing the situation. Ivan chose to wait several weeks before releasing the results—and then did so with only summary information that made the situation sound better than it was. In addition, Ivan used the letterhead of the department that administered the survey to deliver the less than forthright information without the permission of the manager.

Once the full story became known, Ivan chose to take a demotion.

Purging the Competition

The practice of removing or impugning the character of employees who have the skills to potentially take over a leader's position.

Healthy and Normal Function

The board of directors ensures a system of checks and balances for making important resource and personnel decisions. Leaders who are hired have impressive credentials as well as appropriate self-esteem, and they are secure enough to consistently hire the best employees to assist them in achieving the mission and goals of the company.

Causes of Dysfunction

- personal insecurity
- general recognition that others are more qualified than the leader
- unethical obsession with reaching and retaining a leadership position at all costs

Risk to the Organization

This disease typically presents itself when a leader is chosen who does not possess the requisite skills to adequately perform his or her job duties. The risk is that the leader will choose the protection of the loyally incompetent to cover over his or her deficiencies rather than retaining qualified staff to help him or her. The leader focuses more on the negative possibility of having to constantly look over his or her shoulder and be second-guessed than the positive possibility of gaining recognition and praise for hiring and listening to competent advisers.

Symptoms and Signs

- near-dictatorial power given to the leader
- leader's obsession that everyone in the organization must acknowledge his or her authority
- inner decision-making circle comprised of less-qualified employees
- increased number of complaints filed claiming adverse employment actions taken without just cause
- rumors that a significant organizational structure change is imminent

Diagnostic Analysis

- Have good employees unexpectedly resigned or been terminated with little or no explanation given?
- Does the leader exert total dominance over the organization?
- Is there a lack of remorse from the leader when letting qualified individuals go?
- Is the leader's bravado camouflaging his or her low self-esteem?
- Is dominance or intimidation used to control others?
- Have public statements been used to systematically damage the reputation of a credible employee who can't be summarily dismissed?

Progression and Impact

In order to implement a purge, a leader needs to have complete authority from the board of directors to run the organization in any way he or she sees fit. Once the leader obtains this degree of power, he or she is free to plan the removal of anyone who could pose a threat to his or her rule. This is either done quickly through a coordinated purge or over time through the malicious impugning of an employee's reputation or the continual harassment of employees until they experience enough stress to "voluntarily" leave the organization.

When this occurs, there is a free fall in employee morale, accompanied by significant apprehension over the exploitation of supervisory boundaries. Experienced employees are bounced in favor of less qualified or unknown newcomers. These replacements begin the propaganda campaign of the new regime, which proclaims a new mission and goals for the organization. It is made clear that all employees must be in step with the new ways of doing and seeing things. Compliance is mandatory and rewarded; noncompliance is futile and punished. Employees either assimilate or are labeled as uniquely unqualified to stay. The most important employee attribute becomes loyalty to the insecure leader and his or her work program.

Prognosis

The success or failure of an organization is predicated upon the quality of decisions made by its leaders and the ability of the workforce to implement those decisions efficiently and effectively. With this disease, the organization irrationally purges the talent that would allow it to be a sustainable enterprise. Mediocrity is inevitable.

Treatment or Cure

- The board of directors sets policy and monitors its efficient, effective, and ethical implementation.
- Approval systems are set up for discussion of important decisions, such as changing the organizational structure, budget, and personnel.
- Applicants are selected and retained based on merit rather than the non-vetted whims of any one person.
- The board of directors cultivates appropriate professional relationships with key staff so they can stay abreast of critical operational and personnel issues and are not limited to solely assessing the organization based on the CEO's perspective.

Case Study

The Bitter Bunch

Michelle was a significantly under-qualified individual who was backed by the political elite of the community to run for an elected office. After winning the election and taking office, Michelle summarily and maliciously dismissed longtime productive employees, replacing them with under-qualified and malcontented ones who had been previously passed over because of their limited skill sets. This "bitter bunch" began to secure their power base through fear and intimidation so that no one would question their predictably poor future decisions.

Michelle also sought to expand her power base by attempted program grabs from other departments. Those who questioned her approach were targeted for retaliation by having their personnel files and economic transactions scrutinized for any signs of irregularity. This went as far as Michelle meddling in and making decisions on issues beyond the scope of her authority.

Eventually, Michelle was removed from her position, and the organization floundered for months while the bitter bunch was replaced by a better bunch. Meanwhile, the unqualified and obnoxious second-in-command held the fort down (and underwater) until a qualified replacement could be found to bring normalcy back to the organization.

Speaking without Saying Anything

The ability to sound authoritative on any work subject—yet when one is finished speaking, no one really knows what was said.

Healthy and Normal Function

Managers "walk the talk"—they say what they mean and mean what they say. Leadership ensures that managers have the ability to effectively communicate cogent information on issues of legitimate importance to the organization.

Causes of Dysfunction

- trying to satisfy multiple bosses with multiple agendas
- fear of discovery that one really doesn't have a total grasp on the core subject matter of one's job
- seeing this approach working and being rewarded in the organization
- changing societal values of knowing a little about a lot rather than a lot about a little
- thrill of seeing if one can pull it off

Risk to the Organization

The primary risk of this disease is connected to the organizational placement of the jabber-talky (JT). If the JT is in a critical position, someone has to serve as the universal translator, or else those with expertise or self-esteem who really do know what they are talking about will eventually show up to call out the habitual hyperbole. Allowing the JT wide latitude risks reputational damage to the organization once the curtain is pulled back. The risk increases without adequate supervision of the JT.

Symptoms and Signs

- ability to talk easily and endlessly, with very few specifics
- being comfortable in any crowd or situation
- preparing at the last second for everything

- double-booking meetings all day long, coming in late, and leaving early to avoid being trapped into providing details
- speeches that leave audiences amused but confused

Diagnostic Analysis

- Is the individual's speech full of vague, circumstantial, elaborate, metaphorical content?
- Does the individual speak without much in the way of notes?
- Do his or her speeches hold up to fact-checking?
- How many words are used to answer a simple "yes" or "no" question?
- Does the individual avoid staying very long in any one place?
- Is the individual comfortable with exaggerating personal abilities?

Progression and Impact

Fortunately, this disease is usually not contagious. It is a rare skill to be able to grift one's way up the organization, avoiding potholes and speed bumps. One also has to have a bit of natural luck to be unavailable at just the right times, to deflect the tough stuff to others without calling attention to it, and to generally be a likeable person who avoids suspicion.

So how much damage can a JT do to the organization? Usually not that much, as JTs tend to have this covered as well. They know their disease and ensure that they hire plenty of smart people to give them freedom of creativity and absenteeism. JTs are typically very smart themselves and can mix collages of unrelated information into new and elegant verbal meals to be devoured by the less discerning.

If the JT would devote half of his or her time to accumulating *real* knowledge rather than manufacturing and scheming, he or she would know the material. But that would be too much work—as if making up stories without getting caught isn't. Fortunately, JTs are typically not malicious at heart; at their core, they are fun-loving. They really don't want to hurt the organization and will try to put backstops in place to mitigate their deficiencies.

Prognosis

If a JT can be identified and kept somewhere below the top of the organization, in all probability things will work out. Bear in mind that JTs do have a gift that can become quite useful when dealing with the board of directors. After all, in some cases, they do speak the same language.

Treatment or Cure

- Don't allow a JT to become the CEO.
- Strategically use the JT's skills as the need arises.
- Have a universal translator.
- Have a boss who realizes and recognizes the JT's large deviations from reality and keeps everything within acceptable parameters.
- Don't allow the JT to be the lead worker on a core project.
- Send the JT to training to make the exaggerations a reality.

Case Study

Flimflam Man

Blake was a JT who rose through the ranks of an organization by being affable, agreeing with everyone (individually), using big industry-specific words, name-dropping, and having a big laugh. Blake loved to speak to crowds for short periods to bedazzle and bewitch them with the latest terminology and ensure them that everything was going well. When Blake was asked questions, the answer was nearly always yes, with a quick glance to staff to let them know they now had to find a way to make that answer truthful.

Nearly every time Blake was done speaking or answering questions at a meeting, one could hear people faintly saying, "That was a nice speech, but I'm not quite sure what he meant by that." To keep from being pinned down, Blake changed jobs every few years, which only served to make it appear that he was consistently wanted. Eventually, though, his lack of substantive knowledge caught up with him. His supervisor directed Blake to take a skills inventory and then sent him to training to acquire a comprehensive skill set that almost matched his bluster. Both the organization and Blake benefited greatly.

Chapter 4

Behavioral Deficiencies: Self-Interest Based

The Manipulator

- Exploiting Exclusive Access to Power
- Not Staying in Your Lane
- Manipulated Outcomes
- Noncompliance with Company Policies
- Punishing the Victim
- Selfish Focus
- Blind Loyalty
- Desire for Instant Gratification
- Unethical Behavior

Exploiting Exclusive Access to Power

The leader's exploitation of unlimited and unique access to the board of directors for the purpose of slowly and subtly manipulating individual board members' views regarding certain employees, issues, or projects in the pursuit of dubious goals and objectives.

Healthy and Normal Function

A skilled and ethical CEO and executive staff with intact self-esteem are more interested in customer service than in meeting the selfish desires of individual board members or padding their personal pensions.

Causes of Dysfunction

- being the only individual with unfettered access to members of the board of directors on a daily basis
- the need to garner a majority vote of board members for accomplishing goals and objectives, resulting in "creative" approaches being utilized to gain consensus
- insecure executives
- belief in ability to outsmart board members who may have limited institutional knowledge

Risk to the Organization

- decisions based on false information
- appointments based on loyalty rather than competence
- time wasted by the executive in keeping track of his or her lies rather than focusing on company work
- mimicking of this exploitive approach by up-and-coming managers who believe this must be the accepted manner of reaching and staying at the top
- loss of best and brightest employees

Symptoms and Signs

- placement of less competent employees in positions of authority
- marginalization and exclusion of the most talented and ethical employees from the inner circle
- less face time for the best and brightest with the board of directors—and when face time does occur, a feeling that the relationship has changed for the worse
- comments of the best and brightest dismissed in favor of anecdotal, elementary, non-evidence-based solutions
- pay raises for the loyally incompetent only
- subtle encouragement of talented/ethical employees to leave the organization, ostensibly because one board member doesn't care for them

Diagnostic Analysis

- What are the leader's qualifications for a position of authority?
- Did board members' perceptions change regarding certain talented and ethical employees due to comments made by the leader?

- Has the board's time with certain executives dramatically decreased?
- Does the leader exhibit a lack of remorse for falsely impugning another's character to get his or her way?
- Does the leader rely on underhanded tactics to influence or control others?
- Is there frequent use of charm or ingratiation to achieve the leader's own ends?
- Are dishonesty, embellishment, or fabrication commonly employed when the leader is relating events?

Progression and Impact

Typically, no one other than the highest executives, particularly the CEO, have unlimited access to the board of directors and trustees. When this is coupled with the "adoption" factor of the CEO being the board's selection, there is an inherent trust between the two parties. After all, if the board made the choice, it couldn't have been wrong.

After a short period of time, CEOs may realize that this unlimited access can be used to their advantage. If this disease takes root, CEOs may decide to fabricate information about people they don't care for or who threaten them. If the slow-drip approach is used, a very subtle and deliberate form of character assassination occurs. Even if only a fraction of what is said is believed, over time it accomplishes its malicious intent, and board members become suspicious of an employee without the employee ever knowing why. Every time these employees meet with the board, it seems they have to prove themselves again and again, even though they have always been steady and reliable producers.

This strategy is particularly effective when the CEO (wrongly) perceives very talented and ethical employees as a threat. The employees' ethics make it hard to manipulate them to recommend or implement purely political decisions that do not adhere to the organization's mission. The CEO eventually becomes frustrated with having to periodically convince these ethical employees to overlook the rightness or wrongness of issues. The CEO also begins to resent the talent and forthrightness of these employees, as they are everything the CEO is not.

Eventually, in the mind of the CEO, it would be much easier if the talented, ethical employees were to leave the organization. However, the employees' talents have made them well known and respected among board members, so a direct frontal assault won't work. Thus, the approach of slowly manipulating board members' views over time commences.

When and if a talented and ethical employee confronts the CEO, the CEO denies everything and tries to make the employee feel paranoid. After all, how is the employee going to confirm what is going on? Is he or she going to contact board members and ask if the CEO is telling the truth? If wrong, this approach is fatal.

Now that the CEO knows the employee is suspicious, the game goes underground and is played out using even more subtle tactics. In the end, the employee has very few options and too many obstacles to overcome. When the slow-drip approach works, it becomes a useful tool for the CEO to employ in other situations.

Prognosis

This issue begins and ends with the C-suite. The less qualified individual executives are, the more likely they are to implement ineffective and inefficient solutions that lose the company money or result in poor customer service. Conversely, if the board realizes its mistake with the CEO and addresses it by hiring a solid and ethical leader, the organization will have a chance to slowly rebound.

Treatment or Cure

- Hire an ethical and competent CEO and executive staff.
- Don't give up on the best and brightest until evidence-based proof is offered against them. Require the CEO to provide that evidence or refrain from making derogatory comments.
- Ask the best and brightest their opinion on what is happening.

Case Study

Poison Pill

Jonas self-selected out of a particular part of a large organization because its leader, Cathy, was unethical, obnoxious and malicious. Jonas did this quietly without saying a word about the conditions that caused him to transfer.

Unfortunately, Cathy could not accept that one of her best employees had left the fold, and she decided that Jonas must be punished. Even more unfortunate was that much of the work Jonas was performing in his new assignment had to be approved by Cathy. Knowing that Jonas was universally recognized for his quality work, the jilted Cathy began the slow negative drip campaign:

"Boy, Jonas has always done great work, but he missed a few things this time. I'm sure he'll get it right next time."

"Wow, this is not like Jonas. A second subpar effort. I'll have to call his new supervisor and let them know that in the future better work needs to be submitted."

"There must be some personal problems going on, because Jonas is in a funk and I don't think he can recover."

"Do you think he needs a leave of absence to sort things out?"

Jonas eventually filed a harassment claim against Cathy which the organization attempted to bury over a two-year period of time. Eventually, however, Cathy couldn't recover from the myriad of retaliatory behaviors she had participated in with several other employees, and she was quietly asked to leave the organization.

Not Staying in Your Lane

The inability or refusal to operate within the boundaries of one's assignment or job duties.

Healthy and Normal Function

The CEO and executives work well together as a team, recognizing and respecting each other's spheres of authority. Executives recognize the value of staying within their individual roles so the organization can function cohesively and ethically. When changes to the organization need to be made, they are discussed openly, and consensus is reached before moving forward.

Causes of Dysfunction

- ego
- lust for power
- belief that no one can do it better
- desire to make up for others' deficiencies

Risk to the Organization

The risk is that well-thought-out and established boundaries designed to ensure appropriate checks, balances, and demarcations of interest will be blurred or trampled, causing confusion and disunity in an organization.

Symptoms and Signs

- a CEO who does not give clear and timely direction
- discord between executives over encroachments into each other's areas
- reorganization proposals that attempt to expand an individual's chain of command or sphere of influence
- staff taking sides on issues
- new or inexperienced executives demonstrating an unhealthy degree of ambition

Diagnostic Analysis

- Have there been repeated instances of assignments given to staff outside of their chain of command?
- Do employees consistently vocalize their confusion about who to take direction from?
- Does a manager have a history of consistently working on projects outside his or her scope of authority?
- Is goal-setting based on personal gratification?

Progression and Impact

Executives use organizational charts to delineate clear lines of authority. They give considerable thought as to how work should flow, who should supervise what functions, and what checks and balances should be put in place to ensure an ethical environment that complies with all laws, rules, and regulations. Over time, many organizations periodically revise their structure to improve efficiency or change the operating environment. The board of directors typically approves these changes.

Employees who rise to the executive ranks are typically hard-charging individuals with loads of ambition. In these situations, there will always be a natural tendency for authority-creep among executives jockeying for position, power, and pay. When this happens, there will also be a sharp territorial response to an executive who meanders into another's sphere of influence. The CEO must see to it that any unhealthy ambitions are contained for the benefit of the organization. When the CEO fails to check these encroachments, it creates a number of troubling ripples throughout the organization, including the following:

- Executives get the impression that it is okay to encroach, which opens the floodgates to additional internal hostile takeover attempts.
- Employees choose sides in internal battles.
- Instability and uncertainty run rife throughout the organization, negatively impacting productivity and the efficient allocation of resources.
- Damage is done to the check-and-balance structures, making it more possible for one part of the organization to obtain an unhealthy amount of power.

Prognosis

If the CEO addresses these problems early and develops a systematic approach for proposed organizational changes, the majority of employees will view this as reasonable, and the issue will be properly addressed. If internal conflicts are not sufficiently contained in a timely manner, there will be considerable damage to the organization that will linger for some time. Examples of damage include refusal to work with the encroacher, pitting factions of employees against one another, and refusal to share information.

Treatment or Cure

- Ensure that roles and responsibilities are clearly delineated and distributed to staff.
- Create and adhere to a policy and procedure for the review and approval of all significant organizational changes.
- The CEO ensures cooperation and respect for lines of authority.
- New executives receive training that includes explaining why the organization is formed the way it is and what the structure is trying to accomplish.

Case Study

The Encroacher

Ryan was an inexperienced but ambitious executive who took it upon himself to encroach into areas of the organization outside his purview. Ryan would occasionally meet with employees outside his chain of command to "give" assignments or "suggest" ways of doing things, and to request periodic favors. It was clear that Ryan had no idea about the reasons why the organization was set up the way it was or certain protocols needed to be followed.

Ryan's approach caused a great deal of conflict between peers who resented the encroachment as well as the obvious lack of understanding demonstrated by the type and nature of requests made. In addition, his behavior caused considerable consternation and confusion among the staff. Many felt Ryan would not have given direction unless he had cleared it with the other executives whose area was impacted. When it was inevitably discovered that Ryan's main desire was to increase his own power and influence, employees felt caught in the middle and worried about a power struggle in which there would be winners and losers.

It became clear that Ryan just wanted what he wanted and felt that others should acquiesce to his demands. This was highly offensive, as Ryan had an insufficient résumé and time in the system to know what he was doing. When confronted, Ryan always denied any wrongdoing and had an excuse for his encroachments. He would then hibernate and reappear using the same strategy on other issues. Over time, Ryan's style reflected poorly on the organization, and several of his initiatives failed because of a lack of proper planning and management.

Manipulated Outcomes

Advanced knowledge of the outcome of an uncertain future event because one unethically manipulated its conclusion. In other words, "the fix is in."

Healthy and Normal Function

An organization should deal with all issues upfront and exude transparency to ensure that every decision is made with all players present and based on all the relevant facts. Worthy recommendations are proposed and decisions are made based on evidence-based data. Organization executives act aggressively to curtail any issues of fraud or deception.

Causes of Dysfunction

- political considerations or directives
- an inordinate desire for a given outcome
- an effort to maximize personal gain and/or minimize personal pain
- the need to illegitimately prove oneself right
- fear of and unwillingness to accept the implications or consequences of certain outcomes to the organization

Risk to the Organization

The risk to the organization is that recommendations proposed, decisions made, and resources allocated will not be based on accurate information, and staff will learn that events and outcomes were manipulated.

Symptoms and Signs

- ignoring or downplaying relevant facts
- downplaying the necessity of field work given that the outcome is already known
- concocting of rationalizations to make it easier to accept and implement unethical decisions
- increased number of closed-door discussions
- consistent feeling that there is something one doesn't know or that something is not quite right

- unusual calmness and lack of concern over a critical issue that normally would cause worry (because the outcome is already known)
- lack of contingency planning because the alternative to be chosen is a foregone conclusion

Diagnostic Analysis

- Are atypical "risky" commitments made in advance based on the certainty of an outcome?
- Under oath, do employees admit that outcomes were manipulated?
- What happens when you suggest, as a ploy to gauge the reaction, that the organization should strongly favor and pursue another option?
- Are behind-the-scenes tactics frequently used to achieve an individual's ends?
- Is the individual exhibiting a lack of interest in pursuing ethical resolutions that benefit all?

Progression and Impact

If the C-suite is thinking and behaving rationally, this strategy will not be used. However, if it always seems to work, executives may get lazy and be tempted to use it more frequently. This sends a clear message to employees that outcomes can be bought and paid for depending on who one is and what one has to offer. This will result in disenchantment among many of the organization's most skilled and committed employees.

It will also create a power shift within the organization. Marginal employees with advanced manipulation skills will feel more valued than steady and ethically reliable employees. Over time, this more easily obtained skill set will proliferate throughout the organization.

Once the organization is known for its questionable tactics, questionable actions will be employed more frequently, attracting unseemly characters from outside the organization who will want to play the game at a level the organization may not be prepared for.

Prognosis

If this is a persistent pattern of behavior, over time the organization may collapse under the weight of its crumbling foundation.

Treatment or Cure

- Institutionalize a process that ensures a thorough and objective analysis be done for every proposed new venture. If it appears that a desired outcome may be likely or is actively sought, be careful to ensure that the process is followed to verify that the desired outcome is the most effective and efficient one.

- Initially challenge suspected rationalizations by asking probing questions rather than making accusations.
- Ensure an effective and unbiased ethics committee for the organization and submit persistent irregularities to the committee for legitimate and professional review.
- Reward those who demonstrate ethical behavior and discipline those who do not.
- Ferret out conflicts of interests in any analysis and decision-making process.
- Instill the legitimate belief that the organization can survive any situation if the truth is brought forward and honestly addressed.

Case Study

The Three Unwise Monkeys

Howard was an executive whose strategy was never to bring problems to his boss. The first and most important rule for Howard was to declare that everything was "fine." To make this work, Howard could never admit that any of his direct subordinates had any significant problems.

One negative outcome of this approach was that if there were no problems, employee discipline became irrelevant and unnecessary. If during the normal course of business an occasional situation arose that required a personnel investigation, the investigation had to of course finding nothing wrong to confirm that everything was "fine." As such, Howard would see to it that any direct reports accused of wrongdoing would be investigated by a handpicked group of "monkey" managers who were visually, auditorily and vocally challenged.

As a result, no allegations against any of his direct reports were ever substantiated. Instead, outcomes were finessed behind the scenes. This approach worked for a time until the direct reports learned that they would never be held accountable. Rather than appreciate their unwarranted exonerations, human nature kicked in, and their behaviors became increasingly risky and defiant.

Before long, there were just too many scandals breaking out at once to be ignored and covered up. The cavalry was subsequently called in and produced reports that summarily dismissed the predetermined-outcome claims made by the primate patrol.

Noncompliance with Company Policies

The knowing violation and ignoring of policies and procedures for personal gain or benefit.

Healthy and Normal Function

Executives, management, and staff all know what the rules and regulations are, why they were developed, and the importance of complying with them. The organization makes it clear that it values compliance, rewards those who do comply, and takes action against those who don't.

Causes of Dysfunction

- management/executives attempting to gain an unethical competitive advantage by not playing by the rules
- management/executives allowing noncompliance to go unchecked as long as results are achieved
- complicated, overly burdensome, costly, and outdated policies and procedures
- consistently viewing oneself as a victim forced to level the playing field by illegitimate means

Risk to the Organization

Encouraging or ignoring those who bypass rules and regulations exposes the organization to significant liability and undercuts the organization's code of conduct as a template for success. Such an environment can either corrupt those who learn that breaking the rules is a formulary for success or drive out ethical employees, leaving only rule-breakers to lead and manage.

Symptoms and Signs

- advancement of self-serving managers and executives who play fast and loose with the rules
- increasing disregard for policies and procedures at all levels
- increasing number of complaints filed
- disparaging of managers who adhere to policies and procedures

Diagnostic Analysis

- Do audits reveal noncompliance in procurement, personnel, or operational practices?
- Are managers/executives who do not follow or even care to know the rules and regulations promoted?
- How many risk claims are lost and fines paid?
- Have honest managers/executives who understand the value of following rules and regulations been leaving the company?
- Do affected individuals consistently exhibit a lack of respect for authority and engage in risky and potentially self-damaging activities?

Progression and Impact

Once it becomes known that employees can be promoted to a management/executive position by "creatively" navigating around rules and regulations, more employees will be encouraged to copy the behavior. An organization then free-falls from isolated instances of noncompliance to widespread deviation and corruption. In this environment, manipulation and sleight of hand become valued skills in an effort to falsely project compliance. This also increases the applicant pool to include consideration of those with negative attributes.

Prognosis

Once it is discovered that an organization plays fast and loose with its policies and procedures, auditing entities tag the organization as suspect. Once this occurs, auditors dramatically increase their monitoring and reporting efforts, which significantly slows down business activities. In addition, now that the organization has increased its number of unethical managers, it becomes difficult to reconstitute an organization that knows the regulations, values the reasons they were established, and understands how to develop positive habits to comply with them.

Treatment or Cure

- Set clear expectations that rules and regulations are to be followed.
- Provide sufficient training so that employees know company policies and procedures and acceptable/unacceptable behaviors.
- Conduct audits in areas where noncompliance has been an issue.
- Establish a practice of rewarding those who comply with policies and procedures and holding accountable those who do not.

Case Study

Ipso Facto

Amir decided to hire a consultant to assist with improving the quality of his operation. He decided to gain additional brownie points by hiring a consultant who just happened to be a friend of his boss. To pull it off, Amir manipulated the procurement process to unethically acquire the consultant's services as a lone bid with no competition. Subsequently, Amir decided to retain the services of the consultant for additional work. The correct policy and procedure was to put the additional service out for a competitive bid.

Amir unethically manipulated the process, which ultimately resulted in the consultant being used over several years on multiple contracts, with each contract conveniently written for amounts just under the threshold that would trigger the review and approval of the board of directors. Subsequently, Amir's boss was promoted to a C-suite position.

This situation was first brought to light by an anonymous complaint. The department where this occurred inappropriately selected an internal manager to review the complaint who had a clear conflict of interest and who had never previously done this type of investigation. Predictably, the investigation concluded that no rules were violated. This conclusion was submitted to the proper authorities, who reviewed it and determined that the investigation was inadequate on its face. Professional auditors were brought in to perform a legitimate investigation. The subsequent investigative report revealed clear favoritism, a violation of purchasing practices, and potential criminal infractions. In response, the organization rationalized the behavior and refused to take disciplinary action, presumably because of the embarrassment of Amir's former boss now serving in the C-suite.

As time went on, this department was the subject of multiple investigations that demonstrated clear violations of rules and regulations that were reported on in the media. The department head was eventually fired. Amir quickly retired and was unavailable for comment.

Punishing the Victim

The taking of adversarial employment action against the victim of workplace abuse rather than appropriately dealing with the perpetrator.

Healthy and Normal Function

A healthy organization uniformly deals in facts and truth. Once a proper investigation is completed, there should never be any confusion about who the victim is and who the perpetrator is, and both should be treated accordingly. Those who knowingly punish their victims should be dealt with appropriately.

Causes of Dysfunction

- lack of courage to appropriately address the issue
- easier to falsely blame the victim than to admit culpability for the abuse
- organizational power of the perpetrator greater than that of the victim
- organization does not want to make restitution so will admit no wrongdoing

Risk to the Organization

There are a number of risks associated with power brokers being willing to ignore or sacrifice victimized employees. These include lawsuits, exodus of good employees, reputational damage, loss of market share, regulatory scrutiny, low morale, and decreases in productivity—as well as it just being plain wrong.

Symptoms and Signs

- victims encouraged to leave the organization
- sudden appearance of internal fluff pieces on the perpetrator's value to the organization
- lack of disciplinary action against the perpetrator and, more disturbing, a closing of ranks to protect the perpetrator
- smearing of the victim's reputation
- victim's sudden loss of friends within the organization, as no one wants to be seen or associated with the victim given the negative ramifications

Diagnostic Analysis

- Has a proper investigation been conducted? What are the findings?
- Is management's time spent behind closed doors directed at avoiding culpability or in developing strategies to address the dysfunction identified?
- Does the personnel record of the perpetrator indicate any previous disciplinary action?
- Have there been any recent adverse changes in the victim's pay or position following the abuse?
- Does the perpetrator lack feelings of guilt or remorse about hurting others?

Progression and Impact

This behavior should be a rare occurrence within an organization. However, if it occurs once, even that is too much. Making the victim the criminal is morally wrong and corrupts the culture of the organization. If this occurs and strong reformative action is not taken, it will negatively reverberate throughout the organization and increase the likelihood of damage from its expected repetition. If leaders at the top know they can get away with bad behavior and see to it that victims are punished if they complain, there will be very few employees willing to challenge authority, even when unethical actions occur.

Prognosis

This disease is either quickly curable or will aggressively spread. If dealt with quickly and fairly, the organization may not only recover but learn from its mistakes by recognizing and remediating its wrongdoing. If not addressed, the risk of financial liability, the exodus of the best employees, and the demonization of the culture increases dramatically.

Treatment or Cure

False accusations make the victim pay twice and can never be tolerated. If this occurs, immediate discipline must be carried out—the most likely action being the termination of the perpetrator. It is equally important to ensure a cure that restores the monetary and reputational damage done to the victim. The organization must make a statement that it does not condone this type of behavior and that if it does occur, the organization will make amends to those victimized.

Case Study

Stress Fracture

An all too frequent example of punishing the victim occurs when an employee is punished because his or her complaint implicates an executive or board member. In many such cases, the high-level perpetrator complains to the supervisor when an employee will not look the other way when the executive or board member wants to operate outside the rules. Of course, the employee is right in following company policy, and this fact is tactfully explained to the perpetrator. However, the perpetrator will not let it go and verbally abuses the employee's supervisor on a consistent basis, threatening to withhold rewards to the supervisor until the subordinate is banished. Every meeting the supervisor has with the executive or board member either starts or ends with, "So, what have you done about the subordinate?"

Although the supervisor knows the subordinate is just doing his or her job, the supervisor becomes so tired of being abused and threatened that every time he or she sees the subordinate, all the supervisor can think about is how much he or she is getting beaten up protecting the subordinate. The supervisor begins to dread seeing the subordinate and wishes that individual didn't work for the organization. At this point, the supervisor no longer cares about who or what is right or wrong, but only that the beatings stop.

And so it is that the victim becomes the one who gets punished. Once executives or board members see that this strategy works, they add it to their repertoire and use it as necessary.

Selfish Focus

A leader's primary pursuit of personal gain at the expense of the mission, goals, and values of the organization.

Healthy and Normal Function

A balanced view of employees and the organization recognizes that everyone's unique skills maintain the sustainability of the firm and keep everyone employed. Solutions are sought that benefit the greatest number of individuals.

Causes of Dysfunction

- narcissistic personality
- philosophy that one should get as much as one can while one can
- rationalization that many people at the top are also only out for themselves
- experience with the organization that demonstrates those who prioritize the needs of the organization before themselves don't get as far as those who prioritize themselves
- seeing employment as a means to an end rather than a vocation

Risk to the Organization

The risk of this disease is that the organization's priorities, needs, and survival are secondary to those of individual employees. If the balance shifts to where there are more employees primarily concerned about themselves than the company, the organization's resources begin to increasingly flow into salary and employee benefits rather than back into infrastructure and customer service. The organization slowly begins to lose its vitality and ability to meet customer needs, and its clients go elsewhere.

Symptoms and Signs

- strategy sessions based on manipulation rather than ethical persuasion
- constant use of the word "I"
- constant craving for media attention, positive or negative
- harsh treatment of staff if they are not working 24-7 for the organization

- taking credit for staff's ideas and work
- redirecting another person's story so as to bring the conversation back to oneself
- wanting everything free of charge
- using work meetings to make employees listen to one's personal stories
- little or no respect for other people's time
- being very angry at people if they don't immediately pick up one's phone call
- expecting people to immediately get over any offense once the offender bestows an apology
- taking offense if one's name is not called out in any gathering one attends
- writing organizational policies in a manner that always benefits oneself
- disproportionate responses to slights
- taking every joke personally
- willingness to betray a friend to benefit oneself
- belief that one would add value in any setting
- belief that one needs a security detail

Diagnostic Analysis

- Does the individual quickly become disinterested in other people's conversations if he or she is not mentioned in or the focus of it?
- Is the individual's predominant need for personal gain and goal-setting based on personal gratification?
- Does the individual believe that the rules don't apply to him or her?
- Would this individual be the main speaker at his or her own retirement party?
- Is he or she unable to remain silent in a group setting?
- Just how important does the individual think he or she is?
- How many times is a synonym for the word *rectum* used following an encounter with the individual?

Progression and Impact

On the positive side, this disease typically has a built-in governor minimizing its ability to spread. If the infection is located at the top of the organization, everyone else's needs are secondary. The egomaniacal and selfish nature of the disease prevents its proliferation.

Unfortunately, this does not stop the devastating impact on individual employees. It soon becomes clear that no matter how valuable an employee is to the organization, he or she is not the leader and, therefore, is of lesser importance. Employees' value rests in what they can do for the leader at the present moment. Past achievements do not build up credits but only result in the expectation that they can and will produce at a continuing high level when needed, which is always.

Don't expect the narcissist to reward another's efforts. Rewards are reserved for the very top of the organization or for people who can assist the narcissist. Loyalty is not a two-way street. If one is a long-term employee and pension considerations keep one on the job, leadership knows this and will play hardball. To get a raise, one must give something of value in return: 24-7 availability, undiscriminating loyalty, a yes answer to every request, and public acknowledgment of greatness as the opportunity arises. If an employee does not do this, he or she obviously isn't very smart for failing to recognize the leader's importance. A pay increase is obviously not justified.

Prognosis

Narcissistic leadership guarantees a waste of organizational resources, as only the top of the plant gets watered to the exclusion of the roots. Over time, the plant becomes malnourished and unable to support the weight of its flowers. The flowers fall and are swept away by the blowing winds of the reality that the stalk is just as important as the petals.

Treatment or Cure

Truly narcissistic people are difficult to cure. However, the following treatments can minimize their impact or be used to correct those who have not quite reached a terminal level of egoism:

- Other leaders must be willing to bring their peers back down to ground level.
- In an effort to establish an open and honest line of communication with the narcissist, initially deal gingerly with their self-esteem. Thereafter, be direct in demonstrating how the narcissist's behaviors are hurting his or her chances for work success, and the consequences of not improving personal deficiencies.
- Create an employee reward structure based on the sound of production rather than the sound of kissing behinds.
- Reward leaders who fervently defend staff members who do the right thing for the right reason.
- Require leaders to feed out of the same trough as everyone else.

Case Study

100 Percent Me

Simone, a city council member, was particularly known for her fixation on receiving personal media attention. Nothing was out of bounds if it would result in getting her name and picture in the media. Examples of her behavior included the following:

- calling staff members at all hours of the day and night to ridicule them if she received insufficient media attention that week
- driving far outside the city limits in order to get on television news stations when an escaped zoo animal was apprehended, because the animal had wandered onto and damaged company property
- helicoptering in on rescue scenes in an effort to be perceived as saving the day
- orchestrating "crying" episodes in public meetings, with staff members standing ready, on cue, to capture the contrived emotion on camera
- forcing staff to ride in her car to events so that she could use the carpool lane (once at the location, the staff member was dumped off at a corner and told to figure out a way back to the office)
- orchestrating questionable witness testimony at public hearings to push a personal agenda
- unethically and unlawfully negotiating contracts behind the backs of other board members, and then asking council members to vote on the wrong proposal
- setting up special board meetings to discuss controversial topics without first finding out if all colleagues can attend
- defaming or embarrassing anyone—exposing the organization to considerable liability—or exploiting any situation if it assists the board member in advancing to the next post or receiving media attention

Given that Simone was an elected council member, she could not be held accountable except through a recall vote or pressure from other board members. Simone's employees frequently resigned from fatigue and deprecation. Her peers wound up baby-sitting her in an attempt to counsel her on discontinuing her bad behavior, and the organization suffered through contentious board meetings and negative media attention.

Blind Loyalty

The placement of persons in critical positions based solely on loyalty, with the goal of controlling the organization and achieving personal ambitions.

Healthy and Normal Function

Candidates are chosen based on their skills and abilities. Board members and the CEO prioritize the good of the organization over their individual desires and make choices accordingly. Choices that shift the balance of power into the hands of a few or one are avoided.

Causes of Dysfunction

- insecurity about one's ability to manage competent people
- belief that this is the way to ensure that the initiatives one cares about are carried out
- need to ensure that "what happens in Vegas stays in Vegas"
- desire to be in a position to give out patronage

Risk to the Organization

Selecting leadership based solely on loyalty in order to solidify absolute control results in a monopoly of power in one person and disempowers the board of directors. The risk is that only one viewpoint wins, which can cause considerable dysfunction and negative feelings throughout the organization.

Symptoms and Signs

- top-level positions filled with managers and executives who are in some way affiliated with and loyal to either one member of the board of directors or the CEO
- CEO who defers to individual board members—even on decisions that are in the sole purview of the CEO, where board permission is not required
- employees who lack the necessary skills and education suggested for promotions and raises
- secret meetings on the placement of individuals within the organization outside of the normal recruitment process or company policies

Diagnostic Analysis

- Are rewards denied to anyone who appropriately calls out improper actions being taken, or can't be bought?
- Do discussions take place behind the scenes to manipulate or encourage certain selections?
- Is there a loyal crowd immune from employee discipline?
- Are there tradeoffs between board members so that they will look the other way while certain promotions are made?
- Are company policies disregarded if they get in the leaders' way?

Progression and Impact

There are two primary scenarios for the progression of this disease:

- *Battle over the selection of the CEO*—In this scenario, individual board members battle to hire "their" CEO. They know that if they can hire their choice, they have the ability to control or directly influence the actions implemented by the CEO. The talent and experience of the CEO becomes a secondary or tertiary consideration compared to the acquisition of direct loyalty. Most board members bring their own candidate to the party, and then the horse-trading begins.

  In many cases, the selected person is the one who is least disliked. This favors any candidate who does not currently work for the organization. As the candidate pool is narrowed, individual board members meet with the candidates they don't know to assess their malleability quotient (MQ)—how willing the person is to sacrifice principles for personal gain. The higher the MQ, the better the chance of obtaining the job.

- *Battle over the selection of those under the control of the CEO*—Typically, the CEO has hiring, firing, promotion, and pay authority for the entire organization. The board of directors, as individual members, are in most cases barred from participating in this process. However, on many occasions, individual board members request consideration or favors for those they know. If the CEO allows this practice to go beyond just a "fair look," then the organization is compromised and the disease will spread quickly. Once board members learn a CEO can be manipulated, they will continue to do so. If a board member is consistently allowed to stack the deck, control will be wrested from the majority and abdicated to the minority, causing resentment, distrust, and conflict between board members. The CEO will feel the wrath of those board members who have not benefited from this type of arrangement.

  Also, once other board members see that one member is being given preferential treatment, the others will want the same ability to influence hiring decisions, if for no other reason than to stop the takeover. Once the CEO goes down this path, it is nearly impossible to reverse it. The CEO is, in essence, no longer the person who makes the organization's choices for top leadership positions. Merit is replaced by mediocrity and malleability. After all, weak minds are easier to control.

The primary loyalty of those promoted is no longer to the CEO but to an individual board member. Once the undeserving person is promoted, that individual has every reason to believe that her or she could one day become CEO. In this scenario, employees bide their time, wait for the CEO to make a big enough mistake, and then subtly reveal that error to their sponsoring board member.

Additionally, once it is known that high-level positions can be influenced or bought, the organization's employees become skeptical of the process and morale suffers. It also becomes clear that the way to manipulate the system is to get in the good graces of one of the board members. One doesn't have to earn one's way by education, experience, or results. It is a much faster process just to know the right people.

An unintended consequence in all of this is that sometimes the people being pushed do have talent. However, once they get painted with the broad brush of receiving their position by political influence, it is hard to shake the reputation.

Prognosis

If this practice is limited to a once-in-a-while occurrence, the organization will adjust and absorb the anomaly. However, if the person selected is the CEO or becomes a member of the C-suite, or if stacking the deck becomes prevalent, the organization will have significant problems. This includes cantankerous relationships between have and have-not board members that impact the organization's ability to reach majority votes on important issues, and for employees who must try to avoid getting in the middle of feuding board members.

Treatment or Cure

- The CEO must jealously defend his or her authority to hire, fire, promote, and reward.
- The board of directors must obey the law/charter and not attempt to act as individual board members.
- The board and the CEO must put the organization first.

Case Study

CEO = Custodial Employment Opportunity

There were three finalists for the CEO position of a multibillion-dollar organization. Two were outside candidates, and one was an insider. The inside candidate was known for extensive experience in various important positions within the organization and for always pursuing what was best for customers and clients. However, since this candidate had a low MQ and was too ethical to be bought, the candidate was despised by one member of the board of directors who was seeking to gain control over the organization through the hiring of a particular candidate.

Before the final interview, the dissenting board member contacted some of the organization's most important clients who were in favor of selecting the internal candidate and maliciously attempted to dissuade them from their position. In addition, during the final interview, the dissenting board member severely berated the internal candidate, much to the embarrassment of the other board members. This same board member continued the tirade at the conclusion of the interview, casting a number of false aspersions on the internal candidate in an effort to prevent the candidate from getting the job.

That night, as the internal candidate was driving home, the candidate received a phone call from the board chair. The chair relayed that the candidate had done a fantastic job, but the board could not get movement from the one board member for a unanimous vote. As a way to address the situation, the chair suggested that the internal candidate see an executive coach to be evaluated for CEO potential and to receive any training that might be helpful. The internal candidate was surprised by the request and asked if the two outside candidates, none of which were known by the board members, were also being asked to see an executive coach. The answer was no. The internal candidate expressed concern over the request but eventually agreed, given the prodding of the board chair.

After several sessions, the executive coach sent a recommendation for hire to the entire board. Predictably, this did not persuade the one board member. The chair asked the dissenting board member to meet with the inside candidate to discuss any concerns and see if a compromise could be reached. A meeting was scheduled on three separate occasions, but each was cancelled at the last minute by the dissenting board member. The meeting that eventually took place was polite but perfunctory.

At the board meeting to select the CEO, there was a slight majority for the internal candidate. However, one board member who expressed a desire to vote for the internal candidate expressed concern over voting for a CEO with only a slight majority. As a compromise, one of the outside candidates was then considered. After negotiations, the first outside candidate was not chosen. A second board vote was held with the same results, and the second external candidate was then considered. Contract negotiations with the second candidate were also unsuccessful. Another board meeting was held to see if there was any movement on the internal candidate. Same results.

The board was significantly chastised in the media and among local powerbrokers for spending several months on the selection and not hiring any of three qualified candidates. In response, the board quickly began interviewing random candidates suggested by each board member to see if they could find someone who could receive a unanimous vote. Shortly thereafter, consensus was reached on an unqualified candidate with a high MQ.

Desire for Instant Gratification

The inability to delay the receipt of workplace rewards to the most opportune time.

Healthy and Normal Function

Employees and supervisors understand that waiting for the most opportune time to take advantage of an opportunity optimizes the benefits to oneself and others in the organization.

Causes of Dysfunction

- desire to instantly obtain a work perk rather than wait for it to be earned and received at the right time
- lack of self-control
- fear of losing an opportunity if one waits
- excitement of wanting to see something one has been waiting for come to fruition

Risk to the Organization

The risk to the organization is suboptimization. Productively waiting for good things to occur on their own timeframe is virtuous behavior that can pay big dividends. Those who choose to force or manipulate a good thing before its time may find that the benefit is much less than if they'd had the patience to wait.

Symptoms and Signs

- badgering people to bring to fruition what is desired right now
- missing deadlines on other important items because of exclusive focus on the desired prize
- loss of perspective
- suboptimal outcomes because of manipulated and premature satisfaction

Diagnostic Analysis

- Are goals based on company success or personal gratification?
- Is the individual willing to accept unwarranted losses to immediately receive what he or she wants?

- Does the individual consistently experience the bitter aftertaste of not waiting to receive things while they are in season?
- Does the individual often act on the spur of the moment without thinking through possible ramifications?
- Is the individual willing to exploit others, and to use deceit and coercion to do it?
- Is there a frequent disregard of or failure to honor agreements or promises to obtain what the individual desires?

Progression and Impact

The desire for instant gratification is a hard habit to break. It can also be difficult to identify in an employee as he or she moves up the organization. If noticed early, it can be addressed and modified to lessen its impact. However, if a leader sufficiently masks this predilection, it can have significant negative consequences for the organization, including the following:

- diminishment or loss of the benefit from prematurely obtaining it
- single-minded focus on immediately obtaining a personal benefit that communicates to coworkers that it is every man for himself or herself and personal gain is sufficient grounds to make important decisions
- unnecessary expenditure of resources to clean up any mess created
- boss's employees may no longer respect him or her and lose trust

Ultimately, this disease is typically weeded out of the organization by pressure from other leaders whose bottom line is negatively impacted by a peer's lack of patience.

Prognosis

The prognosis is good if the disorder is identified early and discussed openly with the affected employee. However, if the disease is not identified or is ignored, and the person is promoted to the top level of the organization, it can have negative ramifications for the company both in terms of lost rewards and the obvious statement being made that the satisfaction of one person is more important than the success of the organization.

Treatment or Cure

- Have a crucial conversation that is, if necessary, documented in a performance review citing specific examples of gratification issues and stressing the value of waiting for the most opportune time to close a deal ("Wait for it").
- Don't promote an affected individual to a critical position until this disorder is tempered or eradicated.
- Apply peer pressure.
- Allow the individual to experience the unpleasant aftertaste of trying a wine before its time.

Case Study

S'more or Less

An experiment testing the principle of delayed gratification was conducted with children at a Stanford University nursery school in 1970[5]. The children, ages four through six, had a choice of eating a marshmallow, cookie, or pretzel immediately or waiting fifteen minutes and then being able to eat two. Of the more than six hundred children who took part in the experiment, a minority ate the marshmallow immediately. Of those who attempted to wait for fifteen minutes, only a third were able to defer their gratification long enough to get two treats. In follow-up studies, the researchers found that the children who were able to wait longer for preferred rewards tended to have better life outcomes, such as higher SAT scores, greater educational attainment, and healthier body mass index, among other things.

Adrienne was a young and highly talented technician who had just finished her college degree. After receiving her degree, she was in contention for a promotion into management. Her boss called her into his office to discuss the promotional opportunity. He felt that although he could promote Adrienne now, she was not quite ready and could use one more year of experience. The boss gave Adrienne the choice of accepting the promotion now or waiting until she had gained more experience and the next promotional opportunity presented itself. Adrienne chose to wait.

One of Adrienne's coworkers, Joe, was given the same choice, and Joe chose to accept the promotion now. Unfortunately, Joe was unable to handle the duties of the assignment, and six months later he was demoted. Adrienne was called in to clean up the mess and did a fantastic job. Shortly thereafter, the next-level management position came open, and Adrienne was promoted to the higher position.

---

[5] Walter Mischel, Ebbe Ebbensen, and Antonette Raskoff Ziess, "Cognitive and Attentional Mechanisms in Delay of Gratification," *Journal of Personality and Psychology* 21, no. 2 (1972): 204–218.

Unethical Behavior

Utilizing unethical methods or ignoring organizational values in performing one's work.

Healthy and Normal Function

Employees balance the attainment of legitimate personal desires with the achievement of the organization's goals. Employees understand that this balance is best accomplished by focusing on others. If everyone is looking out for each other and the organization first, the organization will be healthy enough to take care of all its employees. Conversely, if everyone is primarily self-focused, some may get theirs, but most will not.

Causes of Dysfunction

- desire to hit the personal lotteries of fame, power, and/or riches
- poor personal ethics and values
- willingness to cut corners to make up for lack of skills
- absence of accountability and a belief that ethics will place one at a competitive disadvantage

Risk to the Organization

As evidenced in the daily news, the risks to an organization of employees behaving in an unethical manner are enormous and costly, both in terms of reputation and sustainability. Since unethical actions are usually taken for selfish reasons, the benefit accrues to the individual offender and not the organization. The greater the number of unethical actions, the quicker the sustainability structures within an organization break down. Simple things stop working, promises aren't kept, people stop trusting one another, customers are not adequately served, and valuables and property begin to disappear. Any basis for holding an organization together slowly evaporates.

Symptoms and Signs

- broken promises
- lack of accountability demonstrated by leadership
- increase in customer complaints
- loss of productivity

- employees who listen more to their unions than their managers
- fewer employees volunteering
- increasing difficulty in reaching consensus, leading to groups either ignoring or not working with each other
- deterioration in general cleanliness of the office
- increase in workers' compensation claims and sick leave usage, particularly before or after a weekend
- general decline in office civility with other employees and customers
- profanity in the workplace
- taking home of office supplies and equipment for personal use

Diagnostic Analysis

- Are there eye-witness reports of unethical behavior, such as violating company rules, dishonesty, time abuse, taking credit for others' work, and bad-mouthing peers?
- Is documentary evidence available that proves unethical behavior?
- What does the person suspected of exhibiting unethical behavior have to say for himself or herself?
- Do employees lie to each other for personal gain or to avoid responsibility?
- Have there been repeated failures to conform to established company policies and procedures?

Progression and Impact

The above signs and symptoms warn of the slow death of an organization from a lack of common standards and application of ethical behavior in the workplace. It is rather easy to philosophically acknowledge that being accurately labeled unethical is bad for business and the offender. The offender is simply sawing off the (employment) branch upon which he or she is perched.

Encouraging ethical behavior really boils down to the willingness of leadership to require and enforce at least certain minimal levels of accountability for behaviors and actions in the workplace. If an organization takes this responsibility seriously and consistently addresses unethical acts, this disorder can be sufficiently addressed. However, if unethical behavior is tolerated or goes largely unaddressed, the organization will progressively deteriorate. For an organization that does not adequately address unethical actions, deterioration occurs in the following four stages:

- *Stage 1*—Small acts of unethical behavior go unaddressed, such as employees coming in late and leaving early, fudging explanations of why things are not accomplished, letting others do their work, and taking office supplies home for personal use. Employees with an incomplete ethical compass gauge what they can get away with and rationalize their behavior as something the company owes them.

- *Stage 2*—When the actions described in stage 1 go unaddressed, those who did not participate in stage 1 unethical activities now consider joining in, and those who were involved in stage 1 behaviors graduate to higher levels of unscrupulous behavior, including stealing, regular dishonesty with bosses, falsely blaming others for their mistakes, habitually running personal errands on company time, and covertly using the Internet for everyday personal business.
- *Stage 3*—In this stage, unethical behaviors go from covert to overt. Unethical acts are done in broad daylight, with an unspoken challenge to the company to do anything about it. Aberrant employees spread their ethical blindness and isolating self-importance throughout the organization. By this time, so many people have done so many things wrong, without consequence, that employees figure out that even if they were to get caught, they would not be disciplined because of the inconsistency.
- *Stage 4*—In this final stage, middle to upper management joins in. Leadership behaviors disintegrate and individual gratification becomes true north. In this state, employees and leadership are insubordinate to the company's stated mission, values, and goal statements. Even worse, management uses the verbiage of the company's strategic foundation to cloak unethical behaviors.

Prognosis

The good news is that this disorder is 100 percent curable if appropriate actions are taken as soon as it is identified. The bad news is that this disease can be fatal if not treated. Leadership must strongly assert itself to ensure that certain basic standards of ethical behavior are adhered to. Each progression to a higher stage of deficiency makes the chances of a successful intervention less likely, if not unachievable. If a company reaches stage 3, it can still be turned around, but it will take one or more years to fully change the culture of the organization. If a company reaches stage 4, its condition is terminal, and it is only a matter of time before it implodes without a wholesale change in leadership.

Treatment or Cure

- If necessary, give yourself time to lower your emotional intensity over the unethical behavior. Ensure that you are able to confront colleagues or subordinates with dignity and respect.

- Start at the top. Ensure ethical leadership by insisting on a track record that proves a commitment to ethical behaviors by all within the company. Make sure only employees who are other- versus self-focused are promoted into positions of leadership. Refuse to promote people who are primarily politically motivated.
- Make sure all employees know and follow the company's mission, values, and goal statements. If appropriate, develop an ethical guide for the organization that makes it clear what behavior is acceptable and not acceptable.
- Train people on both the practical and intrinsic reasons for being ethical.
- Hold employees accountable. Identify unethical behavior within the company and insist that it stop. Start first and hit the hardest with leadership. If leadership is held accountable, then everyone else will know they will have to comply as well.
- If attempts to stop the unethical behavior are ignored, begin the disciplinary process and follow it through to termination if necessary.

Case Study

Gratuititis

George was a well-connected individual who was placed in several high-level positions in an organization, none of which he was sufficiently qualified for. To make matters worse, George was delusional about his skill sets and had a deep-seated entitlement mentality. He believed that he was a deep thinker who could expertly opine on any subject and held the aristocratic notion that because of who he knew, he could do anything he wanted.

When someone dared to point out his multiple ethical lapses, George made sure his next promotion was to a position in which he could inflict retaliation upon the truth-teller. Because of the politics involved and lack of courage of leadership, the organization was too weak to stand up to the retaliatory behavior and just let it happen. Eventually, the organization suffered in lawsuits, damaged reputation, operational collapses, and severe morale issues—all because one unqualified person was allowed to operate unethically without restraint.

Chapter 5

Behavioral Deficiencies: Skill Based

The Wannabe

- Foot-in-Mouth Disease
- Inability to Adjust to Field Conditions
- Inaccurate Assessment of Information
- Inadequate Knowledge of Line Operations
- Lack of Alignment with the Big Picture
- Lack of Balance
- Poor Communication Skills

Foot-in-Mouth Disease

A knack for saying the wrong thing at the wrong time in the workplace.

Healthy and Normal Function

Employees who are being considered for the executive level are screened to ensure they have the ability to appropriately monitor their behavior and speech. Leaders must take their role as company spokespersons seriously and consider the audience they are speaking to.

Causes of Dysfunction

- a "ready, fire, aim" personality
- belief that people hang on one's every word, so it doesn't matter what one says
- lack of consideration for other people's feelings

- inexperience
- lack of preparation and/or not caring whether one has all the facts before one speaks

Risk to the Organization

People generally assume that leaders have the authority to speak for an organization. Depending upon what is said, this can cause considerable reputational damage to the organization, negatively impacting employee morale and exposing the organization to considerable liability.

Symptoms and Signs

- a leader who loves to talk in front of a crowd, any crowd
- lack of preparation before speaking
- strong opinions on multiple topics
- cringing in the audience when a certain person gets up to speak

Diagnostic Analysis

- How do audience members react to this individual's comments?
- Have employees filed a number of legitimate complaints?
- Are an inordinate number of public apologies required after this individual speaks?
- Are questionable comments commonplace?
- Does the individual have a habit of verbally letting it fly without thinking through the ramifications?
- Is there a consistent demonstration of unusual thought processes or a penchant for saying unusual or inappropriate things?

Progression and Impact

Everyone makes the occasional "oops" comment. Most people apologize and are much more cautious afterward. However, if this problem persists in the leadership ranks, it can lead to a number of concerns, depending on what is said and by whom. Leaders are the mouthpieces of the organization, and their comments should reflect the approved views of the organization. In addition, it is assumed that leaders will be articulate, say what they mean, and mean what they say.

When a leader expresses a personal viewpoint or fails to take into consideration the impact of what is being said to a particular audience, bad things usually result. This is particularly true when an executive has a knack for saying the wrong thing at the wrong time. If there were a hundred ways to say something, these executives overachieve by finding the one thing that would offend nearly everyone in the room. Such reckless or flippant behavior reflects an attitude of putting oneself over the organization and its employees. Making ill-advised or ignorant comments can result in a number of serious problems, including a loss of company reputation, a potential lawsuit, widespread negative impact on employee morale, embarrassed employees, or damage to employees' careers.

Prognosis

If an organization continues to allow a foot-in-mouth executive to stay in a leadership role, this will eventually result in significant liability. Fortunately, the disease is typically self-correcting. The behavior is so repellant that others refrain from imitating it.

Treatment or Cure

- Encourage executives to follow the general rule that when one realizes one is in a hole, one should stop digging.
- Make known the consequences of irresponsible comments to serve as a deterrent.
- As employees move up the food chain, provide them with personal training on executive etiquette and professional communication techniques.
- Appropriately discipline or reassign an executive who continues to make inappropriate comments after being counseled and trained.

Case Study

Frankenstein

Frank was an executive with an unlimited capacity for self-aggrandizement and bending the rules to get what he wanted. In his quest, Frank frankly didn't care what he said. He figured if he was obtuse enough, he could "baloney" his way through any topic. His bizarre thought patterns and eccentricities, along with his shady tactics and unwarranted ego, all made it difficult to work with him and to reach rational outcomes for the good of the organization over and above what was good for Frank.

In one meeting, an item of discussion was expanding the use of executive aide positions to all department heads. Some executives believed that not all department heads should be able to have aide positions, as they might use them for political or personal purposes rather than operational needs. One of the dissenters went so far as to refer to these proposed aides as nothing more than cronyism. Out of nowhere, Frank bluntly asked, "What's wrong with hiring family and friends?" Silence.

Inability to Adjust to Field Conditions

The lack of capacity to think on one's feet and be flexible enough to make changes in plans based on conditions that present themselves after a project commences.

Healthy and Normal Function

Staff takes part in all phases of a project. A project team is formed to consider each aspect and viewpoint of the project and make a collective decision for proceeding. Full transparency to the CEO and board of directors is ensured on critical and resource-heavy projects throughout the project life cycle.

Causes of Dysfunction

- stubbornness and ego of the designer and/or field staff
- insufficient resources or time constraints that discourage a needed change
- procrastination due to discomfort with ambiguity
- failure to recognize a critical field condition when it occurs
- not wanting to pull the plug on the project
- somebody owing somebody something

Risk to the Organization

The risk to the company of not properly dealing with unanticipated field conditions—such as soil conditions, the cost of construction materials, or the discovery of protected species—can be enormous. It is important to note that the field environment is the reality, not the operational plan that projected what one thought one would find in the field. There is always a risk that the designer or field staff will not concede that a field condition requires a change or that, while the design looks elegant on paper, it cannot be built in the field. If the priority of the field reality is not accepted, the right fix will not be administered, launching a downward spiral and a domino effect of poor decision making going forward.

Symptoms and Signs

- field personnel scratching their heads when looking at the design followed by prolonged arguments between field and design personnel
- long closed-door meetings during the implementation phase of an important project

- quick, inadequate, or temporary fixes in the field to move the project forward that are not adequately documented

Diagnostic Analysis

- Does the designer refuse to modify the design in face of critical field impediments?
- Were records created of the fixes/changes that were made in the field (such as as-builts for construction, IT, or other projects)?
- Are change orders submitted when it becomes apparent that they are necessary?
- Do future failures occur because of inadequate temporary fixes?
- What do engineering and field staff have to say about the situation?

Progression and Impact

The implementation of a project is not an exact science. On many occasions, not all field conditions can be known at the outset. Sometimes they are not readily apparent; sometimes it would be too costly to identify every possible condition that might exist. A design should be built around the best information available, with the acknowledgment that unknown conditions may warrant future changes.

The progression and impact to the organization of failure to adjust to field conditions is dependent upon management's recognition of and willingness to deal with the unknown. While this would seem like a rational and standard operating procedure, there is an interesting phenomenon that occurs during a project life cycle that makes this difficult. Many times, designers and builders are hesitant to allow for project adjustments because of the following:

- Recognizing the possibility of uncertain field conditions usually adds to projected costs, which could result in the project not being funded.
- In many cases, these costs can be covered with contingency funds, so there is no concern.
- The project may not encounter any serious unanticipated field conditions.
- Not knowing every field condition may be wrongly viewed as a competence issue.

Once project implementation has begun and an unanticipated field condition presents itself, the response is critical. If the habitual response is to ignore the problem or implement an inadequate work-around, the problem may be temporarily solved, but it will inevitably return at a later date, only much worse. This is far more typical than one might imagine. The people involved figure that by the time the problem reoccurs, they will have retired or changed positions, and it will be somebody else's problem. If the response is to deal straight up with the issue and document all decisions and fixes, at least everybody knows what they're facing and better choices can be made.

Prognosis

The prognosis is good if the company has an enforced policy that requires transparency when unknown field conditions occur and all fixes to be appropriately documented. This allows the organization to deal with and make decisions with the right set of facts. If a less straightforward approach is used, the company will have intermittent but consistent issues that, depending upon the cost of the fix, can critically weaken or possibly even bankrupt the company.

Treatment or Cure

- Make it safe to acknowledge one's limitations and ask for assistance as needed.
- Educate organizational executives, in general, about project life cycles and processes.
- Educate organizational executives, in particular, about all facets and assumptions of important projects.
- Include field personnel and construction personnel at the outset of project planning.
- Require documentation for all changes to design plans.
- Ensure that the fixes made to field conditions meet design standards.

Case Study

Who Really Dropped the Ball?

Game 2 of Major League Baseball's 2005 American League Championship Series between the Chicago White Sox and the Anaheim Angels saw one of the ten worst umpiring calls in Major League Baseball history. The first two games of the series were played in Chicago. The Angels won game 1. In game 2, the score was tied 1–1 in the bottom of the ninth inning with two outs. Chicago catcher A. J. Pierzynski was up to bat with two strikes. The inning should have been over with a third strike swing and miss by Pierzynski.

However, the home plate umpire eventually ruled that the pitch had not been cleanly caught by the Angels' catcher. (Replays clearly show that the catcher did cleanly catch the ball.) While the Angels were walking off the field at the end of the inning, Pierzynski ran to first base because he did not hear the umpire call him out. After Pierzynski ran to first, some of the umpires huddled together to discuss the play. Unfathomably, it was evident that none of the umpires knew whether the ball had been cleanly caught, or at least if they surmised it was caught, none of them were willing to speak up. Rather than fess up to not knowing what happened, the umpires guessed wrong, and allowed Pierzynski to take first base.

A few batters later, Chicago scored a run in the bottom of the ninth and the game was over, with the series now tied 1–1. If the Angels had won the game, the five-game series would have been 2–0 (Angels), with the teams playing the next three games in Anaheim. Chicago went on to win the next two games and the series in Anaheim.

The umpires were clearly unwilling to adjust to field conditions and make the most common-sense call given that Pierzynski had struck out swinging—i.e., to let the game go to extra innings. As a result of this and other incidents, the use of instant replay gained support and was eventually implemented.

Inaccurate Assessment of Information

A consistent inability to accurately assess the value of information received and effectively use that information to prioritize activities.

Healthy and Normal Function

The organization is able to rationally discriminate between valuable and less-than-valuable information in making organizational decisions. The leadership of the organization is chosen because of demonstrated skills and abilities, which in turn allows those leaders to responsibly choose others. This gives the organization its best chance to identify, weigh, and make quality decisions with the multiple inputs it receives. Potential alternatives are developed, and those with the best chance of success are chosen for implementation.

Causes of Dysfunction

- lack of experience/skill in multiple functional areas
- poor understanding of human nature that negatively impacts an individual's ability to judge how employees will react to certain kinds of information
- poor selection of "experts" hired to gather and analyze data
- decisions guided by a personal rather than an organizational agenda
- stubbornness or resistance to feedback

Risk to the Organization

There are very few organizations with unlimited resources. As such, resource allocations must be carefully made. If leadership is deficient in its ability to discern the quality of information it receives, its resource allocations will be ineffective and inefficient, negatively impacting the organization's bottom line.

Symptoms and Signs

- leader consistently misinterprets information
- inordinate weight given to the opinions of those with the least experience, and the resulting frustration among legitimate experts about not being listened to

- consistent doubt as to the right decision to make

Diagnostic Analysis

- Has the organization been seeing smaller profits and larger losses?
- Do leaders consistently make choices that do not align with the mission and goals of the organization?
- Are there constant problems due to inaccurate diagnoses and the subsequent application of wrong treatments to management deficiencies?
- What do the legitimate experts have to say about the way things are handled?
- Can the leader satisfactorily explain what decision criteria were utilized for certain decisions?
- Do leaders consistently act without a plan or consideration of outcomes?
- Are decisions made with a lack of concern for skill limitations?

Progression and Impact

The progression of this disease depends upon leadership's possession of adequate skills and experience, ability to recognize talent, ability to recognize the accuracy of information received, and willingness to make tough calls. If an organization promotes the loyally incompetent, a decision-making structure is established that consists of executives who are unable to recognize and act upon legitimate information. It is the equivalent of asking Bernard Madoff to comment on fiduciary responsibility, Edi Amin to discuss love and charity, or Joseph Stalin to discuss community. They simply don't have the wherewithal in these categories to contribute meaningfully to any rational decision making.

Yet that is precisely what happens in many organizations. Those without intimate knowledge of the operation are asked to weigh in and give their recommendations on critical resource-allocation decisions because of their loyalty to feigned royalty. This approach predictably leads to poor choices and frustration among those who really know what they are talking about.

Prognosis

The inability to appropriately assess information ensures suboptimal results and losses greater than gains. Over time, those with talent leave the organization out of neglect and frustration. This can eventually result in the slow demise of the organization.

Treatment or Cure

- Promote experienced and competent executives throughout the organization.
- Verify expertise.
- Base executive pay on the success of the organization.
- Require the person making the bad decision to assist in fixing the problem.

Case Study

Voodoo Decision-omics

Nancy was a CEO who promoted her direct reports primarily based on loyalty. All were told that they would be left alone to run their operation as long as no problems surfaced and reached the board of directors. It didn't matter how they ran their operations as long as it didn't become a problem for Nancy.

The executives performed according to their skill level and character. Those with good intentions and skills ran a tight ship and attempted to consistently achieve the mission and goals of the organization; they also were honest about issues and reported any problems to Nancy. Those with diminished skill sets did the best they could and tried to address any problems that arose before there was a major issue. Those with an unethical bent made sure, at all costs, that anything negative that occurred was obscured, camouflaged, or metaphorically killed.

In creating this type of operating environment, Nancy left herself unable to determine who was performing well and who was not. Since nothing but good news was ever reported by the marginal and unethical, it was not readily apparent who were the go-to people in the organization. In this twisted culture, on the surface it appeared as if the unethical were the stars, as no issues ever surfaced. As a result, when significant organization-wide issues were tackled, the input of the unethical was given more weight.

Not surprisingly, this resulted in a number of problems. Those with real skills and integrity were frustrated, and they resented playing second fiddle to those who couldn't make the orchestra in any other organization. Solutions that were developed and implemented eventually proved unsuccessful, causing embarrassment to the CEO. After a number of evolutions of this dysfunctional system, eventually scapegoats had to be created by Nancy to escape personal responsibility. Unfortunately, the inept and ethically challenged executives hired by Nancy were good at this game, having had so much practice. They subsequently turned on the CEO, which led to the Nancy's eventual ouster.

Inadequate Knowledge of Line Operations

An inattention to and/or insufficient knowledge of daily operations that negatively impacts leadership's ability to manage.

Healthy and Normal Function

Managers hired have an intimate knowledge of line operations, or are put through specific training once promoted to ensure their ability to function effectively. Once selected, managers spend the time needed to extensively learn operational nuances, the resources and personnel needed, and processes employed at the shop level.

Causes of Dysfunction

- lack of operational experience
- lack of knowledge of critical path activities
- viewing it as beneath one to get one's hands dirty

Risk to the Organization

The risk to the organization is the insufficient performance monitoring of core activities. This lack of awareness precludes proactive steps to address inefficiencies while they are relatively minor. In addition, an unqualified leader may misdiagnose issues and give directions that hurt rather than help the organization.

Symptoms and Signs

- boss hardly ever walks the shop floor, instead gathering information secondhand behind a desk or in staff meetings
- boss unable to sufficiently describe in specific detail the status of core operations
- employees bristling and even revolting against being evaluated by an unqualified boss
- shop-floor supervisors and employees withholding information from management or inaccurately presenting a rosier picture of the operation because the boss doesn't know the difference
- issues resolved on the shop floor, sometimes for better and sometimes for worse

Diagnostic Analysis

- Do minor, fixable issues consistently turn into major, costly problems?
- Are resource requests based on inaccurate information?
- Can managers consistently discuss the specifics of operations under their purview?
- Does the boss's résumé indicate any trouble spots?
- What does line staff have to say about the situation?
- Is there a lack of initiative in developing helpful work relationships?
- Is the boss easily distracted away from important tasks with less significant items?

Progression and Impact

Managers should be intimately familiar with the activities they are charged with supervising. However, some managers do not possess the requisite skills and abilities to perform their assignment, so they spend significant time trying to mask their inadequacies rather than digging in to learn the operation. When this occurs, one can only hope that the manager will be assigned to a less essential part of the organization.

One positive adjustment that can be made to assist an inexperienced manager is for the shop-floor staff to spend time helping the manager learn the operation from the ground up. If this doesn't happen, one potential outcome is that supervisors begin to compete with each other to gain the favor of the disinterested manager, who must have connections to get a job he or she is not qualified to have. This type of unhealthy competition breeds falsehoods, insecurities, and unethical practices.

Another result of this disease is that shop supervisors and employees take advantage of the manager's lack of knowledge, inflating their accomplishments, asking for resources beyond what is needed, manufacturing falsehoods so they can attend conferences in nice locales, advocating for unwarranted pay increases, and much more. A worse result is that the new boss tries to hide his or her inadequacies by attempting to gain control over the organization in a heavy-handed manner. Naturally, line supervisors and employees resent being told what to do by an unqualified boss and revolt.

Over time, the organization fails to gain an accurate picture of the quality of its operations. When a problem does occur, supervisors downplay its extent, inflate their requests for what is needed to fix the problem, or complain as a group up the chain of command. Tensions begin to mount over the choice of the unqualified manager. Those who inappropriately favored the selection of the manager try to defend their poor selection, while those who recognized the poorness of the selection from the outset say, "I told you so." This bad decision becomes a gift that keeps on giving, as the problem is deflected upward and drives a wedge between organizational executives.

Prognosis

If this disease is limited to a small number of unqualified managers in less critical parts of the organization, its impact can be mitigated by the periodic monitoring of those who have a working knowledge of the floor level. If it erupts periodically or is located in core functions, the organization will suffer in lower profit, poor morale, and inadequate succession planning. Over time, this practice will significantly weaken the organization, and changes will have to be made to ensure its competitive survival.

Treatment or Cure

- To the extent possible, hire the right people, with the right skills, for the right job, for the right reason.
- Identify and provide special attention to core organizational functions that significantly impact profitability.
- Require status reports from all managers to demonstrate their awareness and knowledge of the operations under their control.
- If a manager is experiencing problems, assign a mentor or provide assistance in addressing the specific deficiencies noted.
- If the organization has taken a chance in the selection of a marginally qualified manager, provide increased monitoring to make sure vulnerabilities are kept to a minimum or recognized quickly before they become bigger problems.

Case Study

Peter Principle

Peta, an attractive female employee with an unimpressive résumé, caught the fancy of a C-suite executive, Jim, during an interview. Irrationally, Jim assumed intelligence was a companion trait to Peta's physical beauty. At the interview, Jim's smitten condition made Peta's words and delivery sound like honey to a bear, ants to an anteater, or blood to a vampire. Jim's euphoria reached delusional proportions as he tried to promote her as a peer in the C-suite. The others on the interview panel marveled at Jim's lack of objectivity. Napkins were passed so he could wipe off the saliva.

Although Peta did not land the C-suite job, Jim helped her get another executive job in another part of the organization in which she had absolutely no background. The new assignment was in a critical, technically rich environment predominated by male workers. In less than a year, Peta alienated nearly her entire staff as she exuded management prowess where there was none and claimed proficiency in a subject that takes years to master. Her feigned superiority over her working-class subordinates only served to infuriate them, as they resented being chastised by someone who had no idea what she was talking about. During this time, Peta was also discovered to be falsifying documents to cover up her errors on important projects that were behind schedule.

Peta was eventually demoted and shortly thereafter left the organization. In the process, Jim's involvement in ensuring the promotion of an unqualified manager damaged his credibility and caused discord between executives over the painful and predictable outcome of a bad decision. Meanwhile, quality employees retired rather than continuing to work with Peta, and she moved on to another organization with an inflated résumé.

Lack of Alignment with the Big Picture

The inability or refusal to internalize and accept the strategic direction provided by the organization's mission and goal statements. This results in decisions made and actions taken that are unaligned with the stated purpose of the organization.

Healthy and Normal Function

Leaders have the requisite skills to make critical decisions that align the use of personnel and resources with the organization's mission and goals. When poor choices or strategies are identified, they are immediately addressed, and course changes are made to right the ship.

Causes of Dysfunction

- inexperience
- ego—the "big picture" is a self-portrait
- lack of perspective due to not viewing circumstances from multiple viewpoints or standing back far enough to see the whole parade
- yielding to political pressure to implement a "special" project

Risk to the Organization

The inherent risk of this disorder is the misallocation of scarce resources in a way that negatively impacts the company's bottom line. The inability to step back and see connections, moves, and countermoves inevitably results in the misallocation of resources to areas that do not maximize effectiveness and efficiency.

Symptoms and Signs

- projects approved that do not align with the company's mission or goals
- duplication of efforts and erratic, uncoordinated movements by management
- elementary decisions and actions that are taken advantage of by the competition
- far-sighted decisions made by near-sighted people
- executives who are only able to see a single square on the chessboard

Diagnostic Analysis

- Can each organizational activity be matched against mission, goal, and value statements?
- Is there evidence of roads built to nowhere or tunnels that don't meet in the middle?
- Has the company seen a reduced return on investment as a result of frequent non-mission-centric activities?
- Are mission-centric projects not funded in favor of non-mission-centric projects?
- Do employees and their leaders demonstrate idiosyncratic thought processes that do not align with company priorities?

Progression and Impact

This disease can have a far-reaching and devastating impact. All organizations have limited resources that must be managed effectively. Knowing precisely where one wants to go and the most efficient way to get there places the organization in the best position to maximize its return on investment. If those at the top do not have the proper experience, the ability to think strategically, or the right motivation, company resources will be mailed to the wrong address. Expenses will at least double, and some or all of the package pilfered in the process. If poor decisions are made because they benefit a small segment of the organization, anger and resentment will build among employees.

Alongside monetary losses, there may be reputational consequences from spending limited company funds on non-mission-centric activities. Analogously, if it becomes widely known that the wrong knee was operated on or that the launch codes were given to the wrong people, it is highly unlikely those organizations would get a second chance to make a first impression.

Leaders must be chosen who see the totality of the environment, know what the end game of the organization looks like, understand human nature, and have a sufficient grasp of the inner workings of the organization to know how all the pieces fit together. Saddling up the elderly Miss Daisy[6] on Trigger[7] is probably not one's best option.

Prognosis

The prognosis is dismal if leadership cannot see or chooses to ignore the big picture. Resources will be misused, staff will become increasingly frustrated, and profits will likely plunge.

---

[6] *Driving Miss Daisy,* directed by Bruce Beresford (1989: Warner Brothers).
[7] *The Lone Ranger,* created by Fran Striker or George W. Trendle (1933: Radio WXYZ).

Treatment or Cure

- Ensure that leadership has the appropriate experience and strategic acumen to properly allocate company resources according to an agreed-upon plan.
- Hold periodic meetings with the board of directors to review the mission and goals of the organization and to ensure they are being followed.
- Spend time on the shop floor to see the impact of decisions made.
- Ensure accountability for poor choices.

Case Study

Tit for Tat

A typical mission statement for a public-sector organization calls for the stewardship of public resources and the efficient and effective delivery of services. The organization's elected officials are charged with providing appropriate oversight to ensure this occurs. One area where this duty has become increasingly difficult is in labor negotiations. In many ways, the process appears stacked in favor of the unions. Some state regulatory groups provide ample opportunities for union appeals and/or unfair-practice-charge filings. Appeals-board decisions show many to be in favor of employees and their unions. Additionally, labor groups typically provide endorsements and contribute money to political candidates. Under these conditions, ensuring the mission-centric values of fiscal stewardship becomes tenuous for some elected officials.

For public-sector executives who must manage these limited public resources, collective-bargaining negotiations with some of the more politically powerful groups can be like restoring order in a riot where looting is taking place. The looters operate under the cover of darkness (lack of transparency), break into coffers (taxpayer wallets), and take more than what has been earned. They take because they can, feeling little or no remorse for their actions or the consequences to the organization or community at large.

In some cases, politicians are notified in advance and advised to stay out of the way, with promises of future booty for personal pursuits if they leave the doors unlocked. The more malleable politicians find clever ways to mask this myopic and self-serving view by falsely claiming their actions are to ensure that citizens receive quality public services.

Under these circumstances, the big picture of public stewardship is disregarded in exchange for the personal benefit of individual politicians. Indeed, public jurisdictions have declared bankruptcy substantially because of approving pension costs they could not afford. This sets up a difficult tension between selfish board members and their more responsible colleagues and company executives who recommend a more economically sustainable approach. Executives must make a choice of whether to risk their career by actively trying to stop the looting or just stepping aside and allowing the pillage of the public purse.

Lack of Balance

The inadequate possession and ineffective integration of a full range of critical management and leadership skills.

Healthy and Normal Function

Each potential executive is aware of his or her own skills and areas for improvement. Executives enjoy taking an active part in making themselves better persons and employees, recognizing that the two are interconnected and will bring value to the organization and those employees who must serve under and with them.

Causes of Dysfunction

- pigeonholed or limited expertise
- difficulty connecting to people
- difficulty seeing the big picture
- discomfort with ambiguity
- incomplete or inadequate view of human nature
- apathy

Risk to the Organization

Leaders and managers supervise employees who have different personalities, beliefs, motivations, and skills. A supervisory skill-set imbalance diminishes the ability to effectively work with employees to gain their cooperation in meeting the organization's goals and objectives. Ineffective leadership results in unfocused and uncoordinated work-group efforts that increase an organization's costs and reduce its profit (private sector) or service (public sector) margins.

Symptoms and Signs

- a one-size-fits-all approach in which viewpoints are predicated on one area of expertise, resulting in an inability to test the boundaries of the possible and the inevitable forced used of tools that do not fit the occasion

- leaders prone to spells of negativity and depression because of their inability to adequately evaluate situations from multiple perspectives
- leaders who discriminate and lack tolerance because of the confining nature of their personality and skill set
- leaders take unnecessary risks against advice of others

Diagnostic Analysis

- Do professional skill-set assessments and performance evaluations pinpoint a lack of well-rounded experience?
- What do the individual's coworkers and subordinates have to say?
- Does the individual frequently misinterpret others' behaviors and motives?
- Is dominance or intimidation used to control others?
- Does the individual prefer to work alone?
- Is one approach used to solve most issues?

Progression and Impact

This is a disease of partial paralysis. A person can usually only do what he or she knows and practices. The body, mind, and spirit of the organization may be capable of unlimited possibilities, but its people-fuel (high or low octane) will determine how fast and far the organization goes. Leadership positions should be reserved for the best—those having the greatest grasp of and ability to maximize their capabilities. Leaders should also know what they don't know and work to improve identified deficiencies.

Humans are complex organisms with personalities, aspirations, and the ability to reason, unlike any other creature. We are therefore unique among the life-forms on our planet. To have leadership balance is to have at least minimum levels of a variety of important attributes—things such as balancing justice and mercy, knowing that people are more important than policies, having the ability to adequately judge when it is best to view the glass as half-full and when to view it as half-empty, having a mix of intellectual and emotional intelligence, and recognizing the importance and proper mix of planning and implementation.

We should think with our heads and feel with our hearts, and then we should search for a solution that combines the best of both. All of these skills will be needed as we move to higher levels within the organization. Those underneath and above us will appreciate it immensely.

Management training programs have spent a lot of time developing technical skills with far less emphasis on soft skills. We talk to our coworkers through computers even though we share a cubicle wall. Building well-rounded people with both intellectual and emotional intelligence is critical at every level, even more so as one moves up the organization.

Prognosis

This disease may be minimized if those who select the leadership of an organization have a solid grasp of who they are, what motivates people to join and stay with an organization, and how to develop job assignments that maximize and balance human potential with meeting the needs of the organization.

Treatment or Cure

- Use effective assessment tools to recruit employees with both impressive technical and interpersonal skills.
- Use periodic employee performance evaluations that gauge current hard and soft skills, followed by the development of training to fill the identified gaps.
- Rotate employees in critical positions to maximize their value to the organization.
- Don't promote people beyond their limits or until they are ready.
- Recognize and make the tough decision that some people will never be ready for management or leadership.

Case Study

Off with Their Heads![8]

Alice was a department head for a public agency who seemed to have it all together. She was a highly skilled technician and analytical thinker. She controlled everything tangible: what she ate, what she wore, how she spoke, whom she spoke to, and what kind of car she drove. Alice was also a clean fanatic. She had to be perfect or at least appear to be perfect. There was no room for mistakes. Nothing could be out of place. No stupid statements were allowed. Everything had to be politically correct.

Alice, however, was incredibly challenged in dealing with people—and as a department head, people were her most important asset. She expected subordinates to think like her, be available on an as-needed basis, never make a mistake that would reflect poorly on her, and never accomplish anything that might result in her feeling insecure or like she could be replaced.

As long as things were perfect, her employees were able to work under the radar and avoid daily contact with her. That suited Alice just fine. Underneath it all, she preferred not to deal interpersonally with anyone if it could be avoided. However, by its nature, public-sector work entails constant scrutiny and accountability. If Alice was ever questioned by her superiors about anything, even if she had been provided with a legitimate answer, staff had to be punished for making her appear to be less than perfect. Her supervisory style was to verbally berate her subordinates, never allowing them to think they could take her place. As a result, subordinates sought every opportunity to avoid a reason to meet with her.

Eventually, Alice was promoted downtown, to the relief of her entire department. Despite her technical abilities, within a few short years, her lack of interpersonal skills with peers and board members caused her to retire.

---

[8] Lewis Carroll. *Alice's Adventures in Wonderland* (London: MacMillan & Co., 1865).

Poor Communication Skills

The lack of verbal or written communication skills needed to satisfactorily perform in the leadership position one holds in an organization.

Healthy and Normal Function

Official messaging within an organization should be cogent, clear, and concise. When the message is critical, have multiple reviews before it is released. Establish effective training programs that signal the importance of this skill set and provide opportunities for improvement. Reward those who consistently demonstrate this ability.

Causes of Dysfunction

- leaders who don't know what or how to communicate, having never developed the requisite communication skill set
- leaders whose lack of sufficient experience at various levels within the organization negatively impacts their ability to understand the big picture and sufficiently prioritize and effectively articulate important information
- leaders with sloppy thinking who have difficulty with logical analysis
- leaders who have a fear of speaking
- leaders with the wrong objective, focusing on personal rather than organizational success

Risk to the Organization

Without leadership's ability to sufficiently articulate a compelling vision and purpose that resonates with employees, it will be difficult to efficiently and effectively accomplish the organization's mission and goals. Poor communication often results in confusion over organizational priorities and direction, a lack of cooperation among employees, and opportunities for those who want to manipulate events for their personal gain. All of these risks significantly extend the time it takes to complete tasks and negatively impact morale.

Symptoms and Signs

- lack of clarity and cogency in communications
- confusion about project direction and implementation tasks

- uncertainty and frustration experienced by staff, with double and triple meetings needed to clarify the intent and content of communications
- duplication of efforts
- lack of confidence in leadership

Diagnostic Analysis

- Can numerous examples be found of poor-quality company manuals, documents, and communication materials?
- Has there been a financial loss from the wasting of company resources and time due to a lack of clarity that produces uncertainty?
- Has staff provided consistent negative feedback regarding the quality of company communications?
- Are long-standing, unresolved arguments festering among various groups in the organization?

Progression and Impact

Effective communication is imperative. It allows for the cooperative efforts necessary to reach an organization's desired goals. Yet despite its importance and daily utilization, skillful application is a rarity in most organizations. The situation has only become more complicated in today's world, with the marginalization of direct personal interaction, short-cut communication styles, and lessened frequency of philosophically integrated and logical thought. We live in a world where we have so many more ways to say things but so few things that are worth saying.

Each organization must enlist a few gifted communicators who know their subject matter, see the big picture of how it relates to the mission and goals of the organization, and convey the appropriate information accurately and succinctly. Try as it might, without this skill the organization will lose its ability to carry forward a rational, unifying, and motivating reason for existing. Ungifted communicators talking to other ungifted communicators results in chaos; the ungifted talking to the gifted results in frustration; the gifted talking to the ungifted results in progress; the gifted talking to the gifted results in success. If the latter two stages can be maximized, the organization can prosper. If the first two stages continue, a Tower of Babel will separate and divide the organization.

Prognosis

The prognosis can be both troubling and encouraging: troubling in the sense that the world's current environment makes it very difficult to learn how to be a good communicator, encouraging in the sense that if one works at being a good communicator, there is so little competition that one's efforts stand out and make one a valuable part of any organization.

Treatment or Cure

- Recruitment exercises utilized in the hiring process should include a demonstration of an applicant's verbal and written communication skills. The possession of certain minimum levels of communication skills should be mandatory for hiring into certain positions.
- Training courses in effective verbal and written communication skills should be mandatory for all staff at the supervisory level and above.
- Ensure the organization has effective communicators who are able to assist in the messaging of important organizational topics.
- Make communication skills a performance category and take the necessary actions if this skill cannot be adequately demonstrated.

Case Study

Gag (Dis)order

A member of the board of directors lacked the ability to consistently craft or deliver a coherent communication. The director's messages often lacked clarity and were phonetically challenged, technically inaccurate, irrationally developed, illogically presented, and—to add a cherry on top—often derogatory to the audience. Calling for a gag order would have been misinterpreted and unnecessary, given the full seizure mode of the audience after each speech.

The director's radical insensitivity consistently damaged the credibility of the organization throughout the region and market, making it difficult for advancements in other areas. In addition, it consistently caught the attention of local, state, and federal authorities who investigated numerous accusations, casting widespread credibility concerns over the organization.

In a gain for the organization, the director eventually accepted a job in another company—which is currently experiencing the same issues.

PART

2

Culture- or System-Based Diseases and Disorders

Chapter 6

Organizational Integrity Deficiencies

Toxic Environment

- Covering Up
- Exploiting Talent
- Favoritism
- Inability to Differentiate Greatness
- Lack of Financial Controls
- Organizational Hypocrisy
- The Perpetrating Savior
- Failure to Recognize Good Work

Covering Up

An attempt to cover up significant abuse based on the rationalization that the organization or the individual can't survive a particular scandal.

Healthy and Normal Function

History is replete with examples of the cover-up being worse than the crime. In the vast majority of circumstances, our worst fears are not realized, so it is self-defeating to weave an unworthy web of fiction to hide a truth that just needs to be dealt with. The healthy person and organization knows this and commits itself to forthrightly dealing with the inevitable 1 percent of madness that occurs within any organization. Be honest, be fair, and be respectful to the customer.

Causes of Dysfunction

- belief that the organization must survive at any cost
- willingness of employees to "drink the Kool-Aid"
- efforts to protect one's financial status
- strategies to protect executives so they will reciprocate at a later time

Risk to the Organization

The risk to the organization is that employees will learn that truth and ethics are situational and can be discarded when deemed necessary. This encourages future cover-ups, limited only by the creative manipulations of leaders to protect themselves.

Symptoms and Signs

- company "fictionistas" who concoct rationalization goulash
- intense, all-hour, closed-door meetings with worrisome dispositions on those attending, including the attorneys
- multiple media inquiries met by unequivocal statements by management that nothing is wrong
- protracted response by management in addressing the issue
- lots of paper-shredding
- no information leaks from an organization that typically has a gossip faucet
- encouragement of employees to remember a specific version of events

Diagnostic Analysis

- Are employees worried about future negative possibilities, such as losing their job?
- Do leaders derive their self-esteem primarily from personal gain, power, or pleasure at work?
- Is there a lack of internal standards that would compel people to conform to ethical requirements?
- Has exploitation become a primary means of relating to others, including the use of deceit and coercion?
- Do leaders employ seduction, charm, glibness, or ingratiation to achieve their ends?
- Is lack of respect for others apparent by the consistent failure to follow through on commitments or promises?
- Do certain individuals show hypersensitivity to criticism or rejection?

Progression and Impact

Every organization faces critical issues that impact its survival. The question is whether these issues are rare or happen more often than the organization would like to admit. It is an infrequent occurrence in which telling the truth and taking one's lumps is worse than "lying, frying, and dying." Smart organizations fess up and heal, many times becoming stronger in the long run. However, as the old adage goes, "necessity is the mother of invention." Human nature can manufacture a lot of necessity when the perceived survival of the organization, or those at the top who believe they are the organization, is at stake. There are quite a lot of things an organization is willing to do that an individual would not. Rationalization feels and works better in numbers.

The cover-up typically proceeds at an accelerated pace. People are brought in, doors are closed, and various alternatives are analyzed. Executives begin vocalizing a looped mantra that "the organization cannot survive this type of scandal." With each discussion, there are attempts to see how far people are willing to submerge themselves into the cold and murky waters of compromise. There are unspoken but understood glances of "I was there the last time to help you out of a jam" or "We will all sink or swim together."

In these situations, if the integrity of the organization is to remain intact, truthfulness must be proffered at the outset, before the stew of rationalization comes to a boil. During this critical moment, someone must be willing to say what needs to be said. The business and ethical reasons for doing the right thing, and the inevitable consequences for not, must be effectively articulated, in the hope that there remains a vestige of reason and courage in the C-suite.

Inconsistently addressing key ethical decisions is a slippery slope for an organization, akin to a person taking addictive pain medication. At the beginning, the medication is taken to blunt the pain. If the affliction can be addressed, the medication is no longer necessary. At this point, the goal for the patient is to learn and discontinue the activities that led to the condition. If not, additional medication may be necessary. Over time, increased dosages of the medication are necessary to bring the same degree of relief. Soon, the medication is more of a problem than the affliction itself. The patient is disorientated, out of touch with reality, overly sensitive to correction, and disappointingly hostile to care providers. Once the affliction is gone, getting off the medication often requires difficult and costly rehabilitation.

Prognosis

When the mantra "the organization must survive at all costs" becomes a leadership liturgy, the door is opened to all manner of rationalization and the resulting unethical behaviors that follow. Suddenly, everything is on the table to save the organization. When this occurs, the organization may survive, but its culture will be such that very few good people will want to work there.

Treatment or Cure

- During new-employee orientation and at subsequent strategic points in career development, the organization needs to make it clear that it exists to accomplish its mission and goals, not the personal whims of individual leaders.
- During interviews for leadership positions, questions should be posed that elicit the priorities of the candidate. Seek candidates who value the accomplishment of the mission of the organization, not the survival of its executives at any cost.
- During performance reviews, leadership reinforces to employees that the organization expects the ethical accomplishment of its goals. The company rewards structure should support this claim.
- The board of directors should ensure that there is at least one person in the organization who will tell the truth about whether the organization's behaviors match their published standards.
- Leaders who are willing to manufacture falsehoods to cover up the facts of a situation should be promptly dismissed.

Case Study

Not Guilty by Reason of Talent

"Daddy, what did you do today?"

"Well, honey, I was in a meeting where people were trying to put lipstick on a pig. A highly placed executive has done of lot of bad things, but no one wants the word to get out."

"Why not Daddy?"

"Well, because they are afraid it would damage the organization and ruin many of the favorable relationships the executive has developed with various groups the company does business with."

"But what did the executive do?"

"Well, the executive verbally abused some of his direct reports, sexually harassed an employee, developed inappropriate friendships with people the executive is supposed to maintain an adversarial relationship with, and lied to the board of directors on numerous occasions."

"Daddy, why was the executive allowed to do these things?"

"It was ignored because the executive is technically very good at his job and was able to bring in a lot of money to the company."

"What is going to happen now?"

"I don't know yet. There are some who favor severe disciplinary action, but there are others who believe that if we acknowledge what happened, it could be very bad for the reputation of the company and possibly expose us to several lawsuits."

"Daddy, what happened to the people who came forward and made these true complaints against the executive?"

"Over a three-year period of time, those who came forward were largely ignored, complaints were subsequently filed, outside investigators were called in, and the organization was damaged by the resulting media coverage and a severe downturn in employee morale. Although the organization did not officially hold anyone responsible, stating that after three years it was difficult to determine what really happened, eventually the perpetrator was asked to leave the organization."

Exploiting Talent

The tendency to exploit the skills, work ethic, and commitment of the organization's best and brightest employees for one's own benefit.

Healthy and Normal Function

Leaders attract, develop, and retain their best and brightest workers by recognizing their accomplishments and treating them fairly.

Causes of Dysfunction

- taking advantage of the best and brightest employees whose character causes them to consistently say yes to saving the organization
- unwillingness to hold marginally performing employees accountable, resulting in increased workload for the best performers
- results achieved by the best performers make the boss look good
- belief that it is easier, cheaper, and faster to use a dedicated high achiever than a mediocre employee to achieve one's desired ends
- when it is more about the boss than the subordinates

Risk to the Organization

The risk of repeatedly exploiting the organization's best and brightest employees is burnout, resentment, and exodus.

Symptoms and Signs

- best employees rewarded for doing good work by getting more work
- burnout and resentment expressed by staff at work or in exit interviews
- mediocre employees expecting the same rewards although they do less work
- talented employees encouraged to take less time off work, or to take work with them while they are on vacation
- upset spouses of talented employees

Diagnostic Criteria

- Do employee workload statistics demonstrate that the best employees are carrying the heaviest workloads?
- When interviewed, do the boss and the talented employees readily admit to the situation?
- Do leaders use charm, glibness, or ingratiation to manipulate employees?
- Is there a lack of follow through on promises or agreements for increased pay or time off?
- Which employees are given the most critical assignments, and how much vacation time do they take?

Progression and Impact

Theoretically, all employees are expected to do the same amount and quality of work. Inevitably, some employees are better than others. So in a pinch, when a high-priority assignment comes up, it is usually assigned to one of the more talented employees (aces). When projects are completed in a timely and quality manner by the aces, the boss gets the recognition.

Also, as time goes by, the boss begins to ignore mediocre employees. As long as they produce at minimum levels, everything is fine. Initially, when the rewards are parceled out, the aces are compensated at higher rates. The mediocre then complain and say they have the same job title and should, therefore, get the same pay. The mediocre know their rights, and their lack of pride fails to stop them from pursuing something for nothing. They take their beef to their unions, which starts the difficult and uncomfortable process of justifying pay differences. In the end, the supervisor doesn't like the inconvenience of the grievance process, and his or her bosses are asking them why all the fuss in the unit. Eventually, it becomes less confrontational to treat everyone the same.

Understandably, resentment manifests among the aces who have a legitimate bone to pick with their supervisor. He or she promises to make it up to the aces but never really does. Instead, important projects keep coming in because the group has earned the reputation for doing things quickly and well. In response to critical work assignments, the aces' character and pride is engaged, and they know that people are counting on them. Because it is not within their makeup to procrastinate or do average work, the aces put on their superhero pants and save the day, again. And the supervisor knows they will and continues to take advantage of it.

If they're not careful, all the work hours and the associated stresses result in a major medical issue with some of the aces, who have literally worked themselves sick while the mediocre have gotten sick when asked to work. The aces begin to reevaluate their situation in light of their health and make personal decisions about where they want to work. In the end, the mediocre stay and the aces cash in their chips.

Prognosis

If a sufficiently differentiated reward structure is not provided to the aces, eventually they leave the organization in search of more respect and financial reward for their efforts. When that occurs, the organization is left with a monopoly on the mediocre.

Treatment or Cure

- Reward and praise according to merit, no matter how difficult.
- Make sure the aces have sufficient time off to recuperate.
- Give the mediocre the same work, and if they can't produce, begin the performance management process.

Case Study

Duck and Cover

The job of an auditor is thankless. One auditing task is to ensure that proper controls are in place so that the organization can operate efficiently and effectively. As such, an auditor constructively reports on any deficiencies that expose the organization to unnecessary risk. Good auditors attempt to do this respectfully and with an attitude of collaboration, identifying issues or processes that are holding the organization back.

Of course, no one likes to be examined and have the reports made public. If auditors do their job too well, it can create enemies. While following professional auditing standards results in documentary evidence to support every finding and recommendation that is presented, some auditees don't care as much about the truth as how it makes them look. Angered by negative audit findings, some auditees ask for the backup material. However, when the backup material is received, in most cases it not only demonstrates that the audit results are correct but that the auditor graciously left out additional performance deficiencies, which now have to be made public thanks to the auditee's inquiry. So instead of being pacified, the auditee is twice as mad.

Out of misplaced anger, the auditee and/or CEO contacts the board of directors in an attempt to deflect concern away from the audit results and to find fault in how the audit was conducted. In an effort to placate the complainants, many times the auditor is tactfully asked to collaboratively ensure inclusion of more positive outcomes in the future.

Gabe was an audit chief for a large organization. In his annual performance review, although he was praised for his staff's quality work that saved the organization millions of dollars, he was not given a pay raise. Gabe was unsure of what to make of the situation. He was confused and upset that doing his job well had not resulted in a financial reward, particularly since all of the heads of the audited entities were given raises.

While Gabe was regurgitating on the injustice, an organizational crisis cropped up. Gabe was, of course, contacted because he was the best at what he did. Due to his prior treatment, Gabe thought about saying no, but the challenge was exciting and he could once again prove that he deserved a raise. Of course, Gabe saved the day and every day after that. Gabe received verbal praise for his effort, but when he asked about a pay raise ... well, crickets!

Gabe finally had enough and left the organization, easily securing employment elsewhere in a company that would appreciate and monetarily reward his contributions. Shortly after Gabe left, a handful of other auditors left as well, essentially decimating the organization's best talent.

Favoritism

The unmerited preference in the distribution of promotions or other perks toward those who "know the right people."

Healthy and Normal Function

A legitimate merit system is in place for the distribution of rewards. This will increase quality performance, result in positive employee morale, and encourage others with talent to join the organization. When signs of favoritism begin to appear, quickly and quietly address the issues.

Causes of Dysfunction

- desire to take care of friends and allies
- attempts to buy loyalty
- strategy of establishing quid pro quo relationships
- desire for one's favorites to stroke one's ego

Risk to the Organization

Playing favorites automatically causes people to say "unfair" and expect that a cosmic force will appear to fix the injustice—it's only human nature. When it periodically occurs in an organization, the company's reward structures and processes are cast in a negative light. Employees stop producing at a high level, believing that their performance has no bearing on the distribution of rewards. This can result in high-level positions being filled by unqualified persons who increase the company's exposure to significant liability.

Symptoms and Signs

- familial relationships in the workforce
- employees in certain cliques rewarded at a greater frequency and level
- ability of the favored to skirt company rules with no consequences
- decline in company productivity
- resentment, frustration, and an increase in organizational conflicts

Diagnostic Analysis

- Does a review of résumés suggest that promotions are given to the less qualified?
- Has there been an increase in the number of risk management cases and the amount of payouts?
- What do the favored have to say about the situation after they've had a few drinks?
- Is there a lack of concern about the impact of harmful decisions on others?
- Are selections made based on attaining power and personal gain?
- Do certain managers feel a sense of entitlement?
- Do leaders demonstrate an unstable level of confidence because goal-setting is based on gaining approval from others?

Progression and Impact

This is a tough disease to quarantine. It starts with a favored few, but those in turn have their favored few, who have their favored few, and so on. Unless contained at the outset, the disease creates a pyramid scheme of underachievers. It is still necessary, however, to retain real performers and producers; the trick is to pay them just enough to keep them and limit their access to the inner circle. In addition, it will be necessary to retain some ethical people so they can be paraded before customers and clients to maintain a positive perception of the organization.

Prognosis

Establishing and adhering to policies that discourage favoritism dictates the half-life of this disease. If policies or their enforcement are not present, the prognosis is bleak, although it may take a number of years before the company is rendered insolvent. There will be many opportunities for reform, but with each step toward favoritism, it will be harder to right the ship.

Treatment or Cure

- Follow policies and enforce procedures for such issues as nepotism, merit-based selections, and performance rewards.
- Ensure that those perceived as being favorites receive extra scrutiny to ensure that they work their way up the system just like everyone else.
- Be transparent with the rationale for decisions and rewards.
- Have a robust ethics function in the organization.

Case Study

All That Glitters Is Not Gold

Sports officials (referees) are, among other things, game "managers." For a number of reasons, the world of sports officiating is typically a closed-door operation that is off-limits to outside scrutiny. Very rarely, if ever, does anyone really know why some officials make it to the professional or NCAA Division I levels. At these levels, the pay is high and the time commitment is intensive. The stakes of winning and losing games are enormous for players, coaches, fans, owners, venues where the games are played, and those wagering on the event.

An ability to manage the environment of the game and abate or at least not contribute to potential player or fan violence is critical. It is not an exaggeration to say that poor officiating skills have contributed to (though are not the cause of) violence in the workplace. Given this tremendous impact—in the age of instant replay—it is imperative that the best-qualified officiating personnel be assigned to games.

Unfortunately, given the historically closed-door nature of the selection process for top-level sports officials, there is tremendous opportunity for favoritism to occur. It is difficult to know how prevalent favoritism is, but nearly any official at the top level can provide examples of officials selected for reasons other than their officiating expertise. Some of these reasons include physical characteristics, such as race, height, and general appearance; nepotism; financial quid pro quo; undue influence; and malleability.

Inability to Differentiate Greatness

The inability or unwillingness to distinguish who or what is truly remarkable and worthy of praise in an organization.

Healthy and Normal Function

Employees are held in high regard and rewarded for possessing and demonstrating high ethical behavior and solid performance that aligns with and achieves the organization's mission and goals. Only those who best exemplify the character, commitment, and skill set required to make the organization a success are held up as role models. The organization does not compromise or politicize this process.

Causes of Dysfunction

- malfunctioning ethical compass
- poor role models
- poor definition of success
- support for expedience and pragmatism over substance
- recognition by those at the top that they do not have sufficient leadership attributes and therefore must change the rules for what is considered essential for management

Risk to the Organization

The risks to the organization and community are immense. If the wrong message is given concerning what behaviors and character traits are valued, it will negatively impact the personality and culture of the organization as well as its bottom line. Most employees become what is encouraged and rewarded. If unethical behavior and style over substance is valued, the organization will be stocking its shelves with these kinds of employees.

Symptoms and Signs

- showcasing of employees with dubious methods and modes of operation contrary to the stated values of the organization
- failure to recognize, reward, and set as role models those employees with a strong moral compass, excellent skills, and commitment to the welfare of the organization

- C-suite staff with diminished character and skill sets
- leaders with high character viewed as an impediment because their convictions get in the way and limit choices
- ignoring of the organization's stated mission and values in favor of an ethically compromised and underground mode of operation
- palpable signs of conscience pangs among staff

Diagnostic Analysis

- Would the company be more accurately described by having a Hall of Shame rather than a Hall of Fame?
- Are there buildings, streets, and rooms named after people of dubious character?
- Are those of diminished character and skills consistently promoted to the C-suite or given the largest pay raises?
- Are high-producing and ethical employees beset by ulcers and other physical ailments rather than the underachievers?
- Do leaders seem to lack a clear set of internal standards and have inadequate exposure to well-run organizations that accomplish goals using ethical methods?
- Are there signs of instability and compromise in leaders' goals, aspirations, and values?

Progression and Impact

This disease presents itself over the long term based upon the type of employees and behaviors that are valued and rewarded. It is critical to recognize that power never exists in a vacuum. If the organization cannot recognize true leadership and is unwilling to showcase truly great behaviors, power will unfortunately be leased out to lesser role models. Employees will no longer shoot for the bull's-eye but aim for the outer rim of the target or a different target altogether. This will establish a malnourished standard of behavior to underachieve toward, one that will ultimately be exposed as a dead end, with negative consequences to the organization.

People intrinsically know what is good and worthy of praise. To hypocritically ignore these standards is to pursue a strategy that is incongruent with conscience. Recognizing and rewarding employees whose accomplishments are the result of bad behavior encourages further irresponsibility and unethical acts. The cognitive dissonance that results from reality being significantly different from what it should be will ultimately bring about several negative outcomes, including physical and mental ailments; survival of the meanest; lowered productivity; reputational harm; and the dissatisfaction of a job poorly done. Employees will eventually leave the organization because they can't look at themselves in the mirror, or they will adapt into a cloister of cutthroat characters with crooked convictions.

Prognosis

The ability to recognize greatness is directly linked to the character and skill set of those at the top of the organization. If exemplary character traits are praised and rewarded, the prognosis is good that the organization can self-correct. However, if an organization has developed an unethical environment based on selfish motives so that proper role models are not valued and recognized, it will deteriorate with the continued hiring and retaining of those with questionable ethics. In addition, the best employees may begin to exhibit a sense of futility and pessimism about the organization and seek employment elsewhere.

Treatment or Cure

- Only hire and retain those who demonstrate a commitment to ethical behavior and have sufficient expertise to ensure the success of the organization.
- Have standards for what is defined as success and the sought-after traits for company role models, such as exhibiting ethical behavior in accomplishing goals, making decisions and taking actions that align with the companying mission and goals, being as concerned about the organization as one is with oneself, and demonstrating a healthy and productive self-image.
- Praise and reward those who courageously stand up for company beliefs and values.

Case Study

Wolves in Sheep's Clothing

In the movie *Gladiator*, Commodus murders his elderly father, Marcus Aurelius, the emperor of Rome, when he is informed that he will not be his father's successor. Aurelius informs Commodus that the emperorship will be temporarily given to Roman army general Maximus Decimus Meridius. Maximus will hold the position only until the Roman senate is ready to rule over a new Roman democratic state.

Commodus expresses his profound disappointment with his father's decision by reflecting on a letter that he received from his father earlier in life. The letter listed the four chief virtues necessary to become emperor: wisdom, justice, fortitude, and temperance. Commodus admits that he has none of these virtues, but he does have others, such as ambition, resourcefulness, courage, and devotion. In a mad rage, Commodus suffocates his father with a pillow so that he, as the son, will become the next emperor by default (resourcefulness and ambition indeed) before his father's desires can be made known.

As emperor, Commodus reestablishes the death games of the Roman Coliseum, and denies the wish of his father to have Rome ruled by its Senate. These circumstances demonstrate the differences between Aurelius, who could distinguish and reward greatness, and his corrupt son, who could not. The consequences for the entire nation are devastating.

Lack of Financial Controls

The failure to embed internal controls into financial processes to ensure that only those transactions and activities that are properly reviewed and approved by independent sources are actually recorded in the general ledger.

Healthy and Normal Function

Management is knowledgeable and insistent upon establishment of and compliance with internal controls in all of its most sensitive financial activities, processes, and transactions.

Causes of Dysfunction

- history of few problems, resulting in only limited reviews conducted
- awareness that implementing financial controls increases processing times and cost
- deliberate effort not to audit financial transactions

Risk to the Organization

Given human nature, there is always a significant risk to an organization if its employees know there are limited internal controls in place to ensure that only legitimate financial transactions are processed. Staff and/or management will be in a position to exploit an activity or transaction for personal gain to the disadvantage of the organization, its customers, and the economic, social, and competitive well-being of society at large.

Symptoms and Signs

- lack of checks and balances that establish reviews and meaningful approvals designed to ensure independence in an activity or transaction
- objection by management to any independent review or auditing of the controls of sensitive activities
- management assertion that instituting controls will cost the entity more money than they are worth

Diagnostic Analysis

- Does an audit of company internal controls identify a lack of policies and procedures designed to safeguard sensitive activities, such as the awarding of large-dollar consulting, materials, and service contracts?
- Do financial transactions violate company policies or indicate potential embezzlement?
- Is there a history of regulatory compliance violations and resulting fines?
- Are dangerous, risky, and potentially damaging activities repeatedly engaged in?

Progression and Impact

The progression of this disease depends on the organization's willingness to establish effective internal control processes to protect itself. Research has proven that the single most accurate predictor of whether someone will attempt to steal from the company is if they think they can get away with it. If executives are willing to follow well-established auditing protocols, effective policies and procedures will be put in place to significantly reduce opportunities for exploitation.

If, however, the company chooses to take its chances and retain a "flexible" control structure, it rolls the dice. As with any game of chance, one will win some and lose a lot. Gambling may lead to a knock at the organization's door from state and federal regulators inquiring as to why sufficient financial controls were not implemented.

This type of environment has several negative ramifications. One is that ethical managers will leave the organization. Another is that the efficacy of the internal audit function will be damaged. Audit results may be viewed as suggestions rather than something that must be adhered to. Audits may steer away from sensitive activities, processes, and transactions, inevitably resulting in a decline in the quality of the organizations' goods or services.

Prognosis

If it is clear that there is a chance to get away with something, someone will always try. Whenever key activities are left without sound checks and balances, the organization is ripe for manipulation and exploitation by unethical employees. If these gaps are not addressed, it is only a matter of time before the organization is unable to effectively compete in the market and/or significant corruption surfaces.

Treatment or Cure

- Establish an effective system of financial checks and balances by an independent source that ensures proper approval and processing of transactions.
- Ensure a professionally staffed internal audit function that reports directly to the highest governing body of the entity. Expressly direct audit staff to report upon the effectiveness of the internal controls over the most sensitive organizational activities, processes, and transactions on a frequent basis, and support their efforts.
- Ensure that all employees are well trained regarding financial control policies and procedures.
- Hold employees accountable for violations of policy or law.

Case Study

Unlocking the Front Door

An organization's internal audit function identified a purchasing practice that had the potential for abuse. In certain cases, a department could avoid having to competitively bid any large-dollar contract by asserting that they felt it was in the entity's best interest to award a noncompetitive contract to a vendor. This was a particularly porous practice that left the door open for significant manipulation, particularly for lower-priority items that received minimal scrutiny. Furthermore, purchasing or departmental management did not keep statistics or assemble any information on the extent or frequency of such noncompetitive and sole-source contracts.

Internal audit reported on this situation and recommended a change in policy and practice to close this compliance gap. Rather than an acknowledgement of the loophole and thanks for reducing potential exposure and liability, the company's auditor was met with two years of concerted resistance from executive management. It seemed that some executives wanted to retain their ability to award large contracts in an expedited fashion as they saw fit.

This practice continued until it was substantially exploited on a politically sensitive and high dollar contract that brought considerable negative media attention.

Organizational Hypocrisy

The actions of an organization's leadership do not match the company's stated mission, goals, and values.

Healthy and Normal Function

An organization continually strives to make rational and ethical adjustments to align itself with its chosen purpose, direction, and standards.

Causes of Dysfunction

- feelings of superiority and entitlement
- a deliberate and calculated attempt to deceive
- refusal of leaders to examine their own behaviors
- efforts to retain position and status in the organization at all costs
- rationalization that the ends justifies the means
- willingness to allow different rules for different groups

Risk to the Organization

The long-term risk to the organization depends upon the height of the duplicity ceiling for executives and the board of directors. If it is still possible for the leaders to experience nausea and mental anguish from their hypocrisy, there may be a limit as to how far the disease will spread. If consciences are partially intact, the organization may be able to self-regenerate or localize the disease to non-vital organs. However, if there is no longer personal shame or an organizational conscience, the risk is degeneration into a pale, anemic organization starved of nutrition and oxygen. More and more, employees will leave the organization and lawsuits may begin to mount, resulting in substantial payout settlements to cover up executive indiscretions.

Symptoms and Signs

- actions do not match the organization's strategic foundation documents
- lack of congruence between the real reason a decision is made and its subsequent messaging
- palpable frustration and anguish after executive meetings

- ethical executives talking to themselves and trying to fit square blocks into round holes
- respected executives keeping to themselves and/or leaving the organization
- pay increases for more malleable executives
- increase in the use of antianxiety medication by good employees

Diagnostic Analysis

- Are top executives silent when asked how company actions square with the organization's strategic foundational documents?
- Has an employee engagement survey been taken? What are the results?
- Have there been increased instances of identity crisis among leaders having to decide whether they will adhere to personal standards of ethics or capitulate to pressure?
- Are underhanded tactics frequently used to control others?
- Are dishonesty and embellishment commonplace and accepted behaviors?
- Is there little reaction to malicious actions that vocationally harms others?
- Do the hypocrites have an intense negative reaction if *they* are personally maligned or taken advantage of?

Progression and Impact

Hypocrisy is a very cool and calculated strategy utilized by executives in some organizations. These executives know there are far too many organizations for regulatory agencies and the media to adequately monitor. They have also learned that people typically believe what they are told. If an organization takes the time to build vision, mission, goal, and value statements that dictate ethical behavior, the assumption is that the organization will try to live up to that standard, and regulators and the media will move on to those companies that do not have such statements. Executives then use the organization's foundational documents to mask their real intentions, motives, and actions. They take whatever action is necessary to achieve their desired results.

This strategy almost always succeeds. At first, everyone is convinced by the fact that major staff resources and time were dedicated toward developing the organization's strategic foundation. People talked about and worked hard to build, on paper, a healthy workplace dedicated to the right ideals. After the foundation was laid, it was communicated across the organization and verified by those at the highest levels. At the conclusion of the process, everyone felt good about what the company stood for.

Then reality bites. If the top executives and board of directors are using this strategy to camouflage their actions, then intermittently these actions will fail to align with the organization's stated values. At first, this is chalked up as an anomaly, as it is assumed there must be something employees don't know that caused leadership to take the action they did. Company executives are given the benefit of the doubt. Then another situation arises where the company's actions don't match its stated values. To combat the building skepticism, executives make sure the organization's stated values are followed at the shop level, so that everyday employees see it enforced among the rank and file. Periodically, when an unsuitable executive falls out of grace, organization policies are followed to demonstrate and provide reassurance that the organization's strategic foundation is being adhered to. Yet behind the scenes, it is clear that the strategic foundation only applies to the masses, and that it can be subverted or ignored by those at the top depending upon the immediate needs of the organization.

Over time, leadership gets sloppy about covering its tracks, resulting in more frequent public displays of hypocritical behaviors that do not correspond with what the organization says it believes. As with alcoholics who regularly fall off the wagon and say they will never do it again or the husband who beats his wife and then swears that he loves her, the organization's outward promises of adherence to its stated values are revealed to be only empty vows. This realization takes years to internalize as employees pass through the various stages of loss, and the lengthy timeframe gives the organization extended opportunities for aberrant behavior.

Eventually, though, employees do realize that there are two sets of rules and that the organization is perfectly willing to throw out its ethics when and if needed. As a result, employees and unions rise up and insist upon an employee satisfaction survey to empirically validate their concerns and force the organization to take its psychotropic medications to control its schizoid tendencies. The organization allows the survey to create the appearance of sensitivity—and buy itself months of additional time to strategize. The survey is completed, the results are tabulated, and false promises are made for future changes. After all, the same leadership is in place, and certain behavioral patterns have been hardwired into a set personality. Leadership praises itself for allowing a self-reflective moment and promises to do better. In the interim, leadership realizes it needs to be far more secretive and clever about when and how it violates its organizational conscience. It goes underground, and the beat goes on.

During this time, the more diagnostically attuned and those without pension considerations find other employment to remove themselves from daily exposure to hypocrisy. The great irony is that among those who choose to stay, the good employees are the ones who get sick and have to medicate for high blood pressure, diabetes, excessive cholesterol, and anxiety to cope with the environment. The organization, the entity that desperately needs the medication, continues to refuse to take it.

Prognosis

Long-term organizational depression and periodic eruptions over the more prominent incongruities are quickly addressed through payouts of increased salaries and benefits. This cycle continues and the organization survives—unless a catastrophic event occurs, such as bankruptcy or clear criminal behavior.

Treatment or Cure

- Create adequate strategic foundation documents (vision, mission, goals, values) that can be used a basis for turning things around.
- Hire ethical and experienced managers.
- Have a responsible board of directors that stands by its word.
- Hold unprincipled, unethical, or malicious managers accountable.
- Establish a robust internal audit function that reports and monitors appropriate responses to episodes of unethical behavior.
- Establish a mechanism whereby all decisions are run through a matrix that demonstrates how these decisions align with the organization's strategic foundation.
- Comprehensively address organizational and employee issues after a critical negative event.

Case Study

Pray and Slay

Governmental entity mission statements typically include business and cultural value statements that are meant to drive employee behaviors toward public stewardship and the efficient and effective provision of services. In such cultural value statements, it is common to see admonitions for the organization to create and maintain a positive, ethical environment that values its employees, and for individuals to exhibit core values like respect, integrity, caring, and trust. These statements are typically widely distributed and often framed on office walls for conspicuous viewing.

The public meetings of many government entities open with a prayer seeking guidance from the Almighty, followed by the flag salute to remind participants of their duty to public service and democracy. Immediately following these formalities, however, it often seems as if all bets are off and the games of the Roman coliseum have been opened with all their carnage.

There are inevitably a number of decisions reached at these meetings that are primarily based on the achievement of personal gain for elected officials or executives rather than what is in the best interests of the public. When these conflicting personal and public motivations collide, there are times when the motives of those who disagree and seek a more balanced approach are publicly impugned, and staff is often blamed for the mistakes of individual elected officials. Of course, these behaviors are incongruent with requesting help from a deity or saying the words "… and justice for all."

The Perpetrating Savior

Manipulating the facts to be falsely perceived as the fixer of a problem rather than exposed as the one who created it.

Healthy and Normal Function

Leaders own their decisions and take responsibility for the outcomes. Their ultimate concern for the organization over themselves is a hallmark of why they made it to the top. It would never occur to real leaders to invent or manipulate reality to create a better world for themselves. If things don't pan out, a real leader truthfully assesses the reasons and makes changes to ensure a better outcome in the future.

Causes of Dysfunction

- effort to create illegitimate opportunities for recognition
- attempt to avoid blame and responsibility for poor decisions or wrongdoing
- belief that one is destined for greatness and therefore cannot be seen as making a mistake
- viewing everything as an opportunity for self-promotion

Risk to the Organization

The risk to the organization from this disorder is great, particularly if it involves a member of the board of directors or a C-suite executive. This type of revisionist leader has no qualms about manipulating and/or falsifying the record in the pursuit of personal ambition. That means that no behavior is off-limits and everyone else is viewed as a tool in getting to the top. In such an environment, no one is safe, and everyone is looking over his or her shoulder. Those with talent will self-select out of the organization, and those who stay will be become puppets in this narcissistic drama.

Symptoms and Signs

- secret meetings to discuss the artificial creation of organizational calamities and their resolution
- directing employees to carry out tasks that are incongruent with the organization's mission and goals while simultaneously making quiet preparations to solve the problems created by this direction

- advance drawing-up of responses for any outcome that could occur
- total distancing of oneself from a decision if "it goes south"

Diagnostic Analysis

- Are there executives whose singular focus is on personal gain ahead of organizational benefit and/or the welfare of others?
- Have those present at meetings where these issues and manipulation were discussed and decisions were made confessed to uneasiness with the proceedings?
- Does research demonstrate that the current savior was the one who created the calamity in the first place?
- Do certain individuals have a noted incapacity to feel shame over any decision or action, an ability to lie in any situation, or a tendency to play both sides against the middle?

Progression and Impact

Typically, this disease can only exist at the very top of an organization; no one at the middle or lower levels could pull it off. It is extremely difficult to call out the head of an organization on this type of behavior, since it is such a strong accusation. The perpetrating savior (PS) counts on this unwillingness to confront. The PS usually comes in one of two flavors:

1. Those who secretly create the calamity for the sole purpose of being the hero who fixes it
2. Those who, after a decision they inspire is a dismal failure, act as if they never had anything to do with it by expending a significant effort in fixing the issue and publicly stating that they don't know how such a boneheaded decision could have been made in the first place

The first flavor of PS is twisted and wildly narcissistic. This individual willfully and maliciously builds the bomb so he or she can be the hero who stops the explosion. The faux calamity must be large enough to be seen as significant but small enough to be stopped in its tracks without getting away from the PS. In order to pull this off, the PS must be good at management sleight of hand and misdirection to camouflage the sting. The PS doesn't want to cause lasting damage to the organization, just to be viewed as its savior, with the rewards that go along with that.

In the second situation, the PS believes he or she is superior or somehow otherworldly. As a result, anything is justified in making sure he or she stays on the throne. There is no sleight-of-hand, only raw power. If a closed-door decision made by the PS goes south, the first option is to see if it can be blamed on someone else. If it can't, the PS must camouflage any involvement. One way to accomplish this is to come out strongly as the "fixer," so it appears that such an individual would have never been in favor of the decision in the first place. If asked, the PS either lies or claims to not have had all the information at the time of the decision.

For those who know the facts, this behavior is profoundly disappointing and disorientating. The PS behaves like a broken compass with a mind of its own, no longer governed by physics. Even more troubling, the PS doesn't even wink during the charade. He or she vehemently denies any involvement in the decision and dares anyone to say differently. The personalities of such leaders are like light switches. One second there's light, and then, with a flip of a switch, darkness.

Prognosis

In this environment, it is only a matter of time before self-respecting or quality employees look for the escape hatch. If the PS doesn't move on to another organization, he or she will eventually get caught, with devastating consequences to the organization.

Treatment or Cure

- When there is a strong indication that events may have been manipulated, properly investigate the situation.
- If there is evidence to support the allegations, the perpetrator should be aggressively dealt with administratively to ensure that these behaviors are not repeated in the organization.

Case Study

"A Visionary Quo in Exchange for a Substantial Quid"[9]

Secretly, behind the scenes, a member of the board of directors (Charlotte) was involved in crafting a bargaining proposal for an employee union that was manifestly one-sided in favor of the labor organization. The proposed contract called for hundreds of millions of dollars of company concessions over a three-year period. In return, the organization received only a promise from the union to discuss issues that might result in savings. The deal was so egregious it could be considered a gift of company funds.

It was clear to insiders that the union had made promises to Charlotte if she could secure a favorable vote. Subsequently, Charlotte hurriedly placed the tentative agreement on the agenda for a shareholder meeting. When a handful of shareholders asked specific questions and made a request for more time to consider the contract, Charlotte surprisingly agreed. In her comments, she made it appear as if she was the voice of reason and wanted to allow for a thorough examination of the proposed agreement, when in fact she wanted it passed immediately. The other board members hoped to catch Charlotte in the compromising position of vehemently opposing an extension so they could confirm their suspicions of influence peddling. Once Charlotte removed that possibility, the board members decided to vote in favor of the contract.

In a disturbing twist, the local media wrongly reported that Charlotte (who quietly had the most involvement in crafting the overly generous contract) was the sole voice of reason in attempting to continue the discussion of the agreement. The passage of the contract resulted in the following negative consequences to the organization:

- far fewer funds available for other company purposes, such as capital projects, equipment purchases, and maintenance needs
- inspiration for other unions to use the same tactics and expect a similar pay increase
- a substantial increase in the unfunded pension liability of the company
- undercutting of the official company negotiating team

---

[9] Ambrose Bierce, *The Cynic's Workbook* (Doubleday Page & Company, 1906), 191.

Failure to Recognize Good Work

Failure of the board of directors to acknowledge significant staff accomplishments because of political considerations.

Healthy and Normal Function

The organization provides praise when it is due—and lavish praise when an achievement is significant and took years to accomplish. Given that there are usually far fewer opportunities to praise than to critique, good organizations don't miss an opportunity to thank and reward employees for a job well done. Leadership doesn't allow malicious behavior or personal vendettas to contaminate the work environment. They use the sour for the sour cream.

Causes of Dysfunction

- belief that publicly vocalizing the board's majority affirmation for a project would open the door for the board minority to discuss their dissenting opinion and potentially jeopardize its passage
- reluctance by the board minority to acknowledge good work from a particular executive they don't like, even at the expense of slighting the subordinates who worked on the project
- too many agenda items and not enough time to discuss an item on which there is already substantial agreement

Risk to the Organization

The risk to the organization of not praising staff for a significant accomplishment is that staff may lose motivation to continue to give the same herculean efforts.

Symptoms and Signs

- no advance praise for staff's work on a noteworthy agenda item before the public meeting (it is intentionally kept quiet)
- board member with unwarranted negative feelings toward a particular executive actively seeks to harass and punish him or her
- increase in staff frustration and decrease in quality of work due to a lack of recognition

Diagnostic Analysis

- Does the board frequently unanimously approve agenda items without pausing to congratulate staff on a job well done?
- Do staff members consistently express disappointment over not receiving a pat on the back for a significant accomplishment?
- Has there been a significant increase in time-off requests?
- Has a need for employee recognition been overridden by a need to satisfy personal grudges?

Progression and Impact

There can be several reasons why a good news item does not receive comment from the board of directors. One innocuous reason is that the board is looking for ways to shorten a meeting that has a large number of agenda items, and an easy way to accomplish this is to pass noncontroversial items without comment. However, passing up an opportunity to praise staff for quality work typically means there is a reason for it.

In the most malicious case, a board minority may not want to give credit to an executive they do not like or respect. In this case, the minority board members would rather punish the whole staff by not praising anyone than to give credit to a certain executive. One way the minority ensures silence is by informing other board members that they will vote for the item if no comments are made; however, if positive comments are made, the minority will speak against the item and record a no vote.

When this occurs, it does great injustice to the integrity and morale of the organization. Good work is good work, no matter who or where it comes from. It is always important to acknowledge staff when they have achieved something noteworthy that may have taken years to accomplish. Denying recognition to those who have pulled off the near impossible is cruel and unusual punishment by leadership.

In the end, these petty displays of retribution hurt all board members who fail to acknowledge good work when it occurs. They represent a hypocritical dagger to the heart of an organization that formally claims and emphasizes that it "values employees."

Prognosis

The prognosis is dependent upon the number of times this behavior is manifested in the workplace. If rarely seen, it can be overcome and forgotten. If it is a consistent practice, it damages the morale of staff and is a poor advertisement for others to join the organization.

Treatment or Cure

- In all circumstances, provide praise when it is deserved.
- Be the bigger person and discard petty jealousies and rivalries.
- Meet with the Board to discuss the negative impacts of not recognizing quality work by staff.
- Have the CEO step in and provide the due praise if the board will not.

Case Study

Medieval Times

Local government internal auditors typically develop their annual work plans for their organization by using a risk-assessment process to evaluate potential audits. This process identifies high-risk activities that should be periodically reviewed to ensure departments operate in compliance with all federal, state, and local rules and regulations. Many times, there is no advance indication of any deficiencies in those areas ultimately chosen for auditing. As such, the condition of the operation audited in many cases is not known until after the audit is completed.

Over a two-year period, one local government's internal auditor uncovered and reported on a number of highly damaging findings: the withholding of information related to criminal behavior, the misappropriation of funds, the practicing of medicine without a license, and the manipulation of purchasing contracts, just to name a few. In order to substantiate charges of this nature, the internal auditor's work had to be nearly flawless, as it would certainly be challenged. In situations like this, employees found to have conducted themselves in an improper manner have nothing to lose by challenging the audit results. They typically search for any loophole or procedural misstep to discredit any portion of the audit in an attempt to call into question the validity of entire audit.

The internal auditor's findings on these assignments held up to the intense scrutiny. However, despite the accomplishment of these noteworthy audits and audit staff's ability to overcome the palpable pressure that went with them, in large measure, the auditors were not acknowledged or rewarded by the board of directors for adeptly doing their job. Instead, behind the scenes, there was resentment by executive staff for holding managers accountable. Despite these circumstances, however, the integrity of the audits triggered the replacement of several managers with more competent professionals.

Chapter 7

Strategic Foundation Deficiencies

Defective GPS

- Inadequate Strategic Foundation
- Poor Organizational Structure

Inadequate Strategic Foundation

The inadequacy, absence, or lack of knowledge of organizational purpose statements (vision, mission, goal, and values) designed to provide employees and customers with an organization's stated purpose, goals, and strategic initiatives to meet those goals.

Healthy and Normal Function

The organization should be "mission centric."[10] All decisions regarding such things as resources, personnel, and organization structure should be based on whether or not and to what degree they align with the organization's mission, goals, and value statements. If a proposed action does not align, it should be discarded and not pursued, even if it's a quality idea.

Causes of Dysfunction

- reluctance to take on the substantial commitment of a strategic planning process that is long, tedious, and costly
- improper understanding of what vision, mission, goals, and value statements are and how they should be developed

---

[10] David W. Gill, *It's About Excellence: Building Ethically Healthy Organizations* (Eugene, Oregon: WIPF & Stock, 2008)

- resistance of some employees to internalize the organization's commitment to ensuring that all major decisions and resource allocations comport and align with the organization's mission and goals
- executives who believe that the unspoken purpose of the company is to meet their own needs rather than the mission of the organization

Risk to the Organization

The risk is that executives, managers, and line staff will make decisions and take actions without a clear sense of direction, commitment, or coordination. This produces substantial waste, disagreements, and a lack of teamwork, especially in large organizations with multiple locations. In our current world, where diversity appears to be valued more than unity, things randomly coming together is a long shot.

Symptoms and Signs

- employees with differing definitions of success
- difficulty reaching consensus on proposals and prioritizing resources
- duplication of efforts
- lots of good activity but nothing that produces a sufficient profit margin

Diagnostic Analysis

- Are there written, easily accessible, well-known statements of mission, goals, and values?
- Are employees able to identify the mission and goals of the organization when asked?
- Are the organization's mission and goals used as criteria in making company decisions?

Progression and Impact

All employees should have a good sense of why the organization exists, what it is trying to accomplish, and how it will get there. It is ironic, then, that many organizations don't formally establish and document a well-constructed strategic foundation that includes a vision, mission, goals, and value statements. In many cases, even when these documents exist, few employees memorize them or routinely evaluate their daily activities against these directional documents.

Fortunately, when organizations are formed, a business plan is required to attract working capital. Business plans usually include a formal mission statement, a list of company goals, and projected financials demonstrating the anticipated sustainability of the organization. As a result, organizations typically begin with a firm planning foundation. However, over time, as more employees are hired, allotting sufficient time for each employee to learn and internalize the company's mission and its stated goals and values becomes less of a priority. Once a sufficient number of employees can no longer recall or fail to use these guiding documents as a basis for making decisions, a number of inefficiencies begin to appear.

If not addressed, the sustainability life cycle clock begins to tick. Over time, employees forget what their mission is and what makes their organization unique to the market. In this environment, employees begin fermenting their own definitions of success, as well as styles and methods of achieving that success. They begin to see themselves more in terms of their specific function or organizational unit rather than a company as a whole. These individual distinctions become more important than cooperation.

Eventually, employees speak their own language, follow their own rituals and customs, and create their own products or services. All of that may be good, but none of it is coordinated within the organization. As a result, different communication and IT systems emerge, and a decentralized administrative function is proposed, making it difficult to communicate across the organization and share resources.

Prognosis

If company executives fail to establish, inculcate, and dutifully follow the organization's stated mission, a number of ineffective and inefficient pursuits will result. If unified agreement is not achieved, company resources will be scattered, projects will linger, employees and managers will become frustrated, and a substantial decrease in profit margin or service delivery will occur. Worse, when those in leadership positions are let go, it will not be from a lack of trying or achieving meaningful outcomes, but from achieving the wrong things for the wrong reasons that provide little to the bottom line.

Treatment or Cure

- Every two years, take the necessary time away from day-to-day activities to thoughtfully reflect on the organization's strategic plan, making changes as necessary.
- Disseminate strategic documents during the onboarding process with new employees, and throughout the entire organization at least annually, to pause and revisit the necessity of making organizational decisions based on these statements.

Case Study

Which Way Do We Go?

Efficient and effective use of information technology (IT) is a necessity for all organizations. This is critical not only because of technology's ability to increase production and efficiency but also because of its significant cost. It is imperative that there be a strategic plan related to its utilization.

A large organization set out to develop a strategic plan to guide its IT activities over a five-year period. After a year of effort and a cost of nearly a million dollars, the company wound up with a strategic plan that filled multiple binders, lacked clarity and focus, and did not serve its intended purpose of providing an actionable roadmap for IT operations and investments. Some of the shortcomings of the plan included a weak assessment of the organization's IT environment; failure to identify goals and strategies that would address gaps in the current provision of IT services; no IT specific mission statement to guide IT operations; and IT strategies that did not align with the goals the organization was trying to accomplish.

As a result, the company was not positioned in a manner that would ensure that its $120 million/year IT investment would be maximized. The company subsequently worked on making progress on other IT initiatives, and it recently went back to the drawing board to develop a workable IT strategic plan.

Poor Organizational Structure

An inadequate organizational structure that impedes an entity's progress in meeting its goals and objectives.

Healthy and Normal Function

An organizational structure is developed to maximize the efficient and effective delivery of quality goods and services to clients and customers.

Causes of Dysfunction

- failure to see organizational structure as an efficiency and effectiveness issue
- lack of understanding of basic tenets of organizational structure
- lack of periodic review of the organizational structure
- use of reorganization as a cure-all for whatever ails the organization
- a structure based on personalities rather than function
- using structure as an end rather than a means

Risk to the Organization

With a poor organizational structure, resources are used inefficiently and ineffectively. Insufficient structure or the wrong structure also causes chain-of-command and coordination issues.

Symptoms and Signs

- lack of coordinated effort in the delivery of products or services
- frustration and finger-pointing between organizational units
- disconnect between the organization chart and how the company's authority and process structure actually functions
- different job titles and pay for people doing the same work
- the right employees in the wrong positions

Diagnostic Analysis

- Is there an up-to-date organization chart?
- Do employees know for certain who they report to?
- Is quality control poor?
- Does the organization chart reflect potential dysfunctional operations?

Progression and Impact

Many people erroneously believe that organization charts are primarily for the initial start-up phase of the company. In a small company, that may be so. But once the organization grows, it is essential to depict and update how the organization works. It is axiomatic that organizational form impacts function.

If a structure is not periodically updated, over time the organization randomly expands and contracts, making it difficult to know who works for whom, who has the authority to make certain decisions, and how products or services work their way through the organization. Additionally, an inadequate structure can create individual employee inequities in pay and work assignments. As a result, products or services that require coordination work their way through the organization as if blindfolded in a maze. Excessive time and money are consumed on working out the kinks—after the fact. In addition, there will be a significant amount of frustration and finger-pointing from different parts of the organization.

Another problem occurs when executives assume that a reorganization is a cure-all or can be used as a cover to accomplish questionable objectives. Structures should only be changed when they assist the organization in more efficiently and effectively delivering goods and services. Employees typically dislike change, so if a change is going to be made, it should be done for the right reasons. It should not be used as an excuse to shift power structures for an illegitimate reason or to justify promoting individuals. If reorganizations are abused, they will become feared tools and be more difficult to implement when it is really necessary.

Prognosis

Fortunately, an organizational structure can be changed as necessary. If structural issues are identified early and sufficiently addressed, the organization will recover. If the structure remains deficient, the organization may experience significant loss to its bottom line from the inefficient and ineffective delivery of goods and services.

Treatment or Cure

- Periodically review the organization chart to ensure it produces an effective authority structure and the efficient delivery of good and services.
- Only adjust the structure for improving the bottom line of the organization.
- Have qualified individuals or a strategic cross section of the organization participate in drafting proposed organizational changes.
- Follow solid organizational-structure tenets, such as appropriate spans of control, clear lines of authority, same job titles and pay for the same work, and logical work flows. Ensure that those held responsible for the work product have the necessary controls over their resources.

Case Study

Risky Business

Human resources (HR) is an imperative function in any organization. HR deals with critical tasks like recruitment, retention, training, employee discipline, labor relations, employee benefits, classification, and compensation. All of these issues are personal because they involve people. People are unpredictable and particular about things like equity, fairly administered processes, sufficient pay and benefits, working titles, and performance management. The government is also concerned about these areas, as it has established scores of federal, state, and local laws and regulations for developing and administering HR policies and practices. Violation of HR laws and regulations are one of the primary sources of litigation and risk management for organizations. Millions of dollars can be lost because of the violation of compliance mandates. For this reason, the HR function is typically centralized to ensure a consistent and compliant approach.

One local government experienced financial difficulty, and as part of its restructuring efforts it chose to decentralize many of its HR functions to the control of individual departments. Over time, the central HR group responsible for consistency of practice and compliance oversight failed to effectively monitor the HR efforts of the departments. As a result, a number of critical deficiencies emerged:

- Many departments began to take liberties with HR policies and practices.
- Many departments began to hire non-HR professionals who would think less and comply more with the wants and needs of departments.
- Inconsistencies in pay, discipline, job title, and training opportunities began to crop up across the organization.
- The HR function fell out of compliance with state standards, and eventually a state legislative subcommittee was convened to determine if a takeover was necessary.

As a result, after two decades of decentralization and its associated negative impact as documented in several audits, a decision was made to recentralize control over the organization's HR practices. The typical time frame necessary to accomplish this and change the culture is three to five years.

Chapter 8

Personnel Management Deficiencies

Management Malpractice

- Choosing Poor Role Models
- Difficulty Transitioning into Management
- Lack of Creativity
- Lack of Training
- Looting of Staff
- Selecting Unqualified Leaders
- Unaccountable Leaders

Choosing Poor Role Models

An organization or individual managers make poor choices in the selection of mentors that provide guidance in clarifying company strategic objectives, advice in navigating its organizational culture, and assistance in developing important skill sets for potential advancement.

Healthy and Normal Function

The board of directors ensures that ethical behavior is the organizational norm. The CEO makes quality leadership selections that could effectively serve as role models. The company's chosen role models serve the succession planning goals of the organization by ensuring the transferability of knowledge and skills necessary to maintain sustainability over the long term. Individual managers have good instincts in choosing role models for themselves who are ethical, competent, and positive.

Causes of Dysfunction

- poor definitions of excellence and success
- willingness to succeed at any cost
- inadequate values and a lack of boundaries
- allowing individuals with questionable character to be in positions of authority
- a warped vision of the real purpose of having a role model

Risk to the Organization

This disorder is triggered when the organization promotes an unqualified person into a position where he or she might unfortunately become a role model, or when employees show a lack of discernment and choose a role model with diminished character and/or skills. The existence of these inappropriate role models exposes the organization to substantial risk by creating and passing on a bad gene pool to the next generation of managers.

Symptoms and Signs

- role models with a reputation for unethical behavior and/or a dubious skill set
- sense of needing a shower after leaving the room with the role model and/or protégé
- high occurrence of cronyism in the organization
- sense of entitlement by the role model and/or protégé
- high occurrence of quid pro quo arrangements between the role model and protégé

Diagnostic Analysis

- Does the role model have a questionable character and track record?
- Are the actions taken or recommended by the role model and protégé unethical?
- Do the role model and protégé actually commit company violations? Are there additional violations they would like to commit if they could get away with it?
- Does the protégé have a poorly developed self-image, with no clear set of internal standards?

Progression and Impact

If the organization allows individuals of diminished character or skills to be selected for leadership positions, its executives are making a clear statement about what they consider acceptable behavior or a sufficient level of talent. There are very few employees who have the fortitude to stand completely on their own. The remainder take their cues from the top. They notice who gets promoted and why.

When it becomes clear that unethical behavior and poor character assist in one reaching the top, such behavior will be emulated. By doing nothing, the organization sanctions the behavior and gives its unspoken endorsement. Once this becomes the predominate culture, the organization becomes a ghetto of bad behavior and performance. Inevitably, this type of environment cannot meet the needs of customers. Rather, the focus of the organization becomes meeting the whims of its "leaders." The recruitment of talented employees becomes difficult, as very few people are motivated to join a self-serving organization that seems to continually ask the question, "How low can we go?"

Prognosis

When poor leaders are retained long enough to be considered role models, the prognosis is a potential medium-term collapse of the organization from the weight of its selfish pursuits, at the expense of the organization's mission.

Treatment or Cure

- Provide written identification of skill and behavioral qualities necessary to be considered a role model for the organization.
- No one should be allowed to become a leader who is or would be considered a poor role model.
- Organizational recognition should be given to those employees and leaders who best exemplify the values of the organization. This will provide a clear signal as to who should be considered role models.
- A robust succession-planning program should be in place that builds leaders capable of serving as role models.
- The CEO and other executives should take stock of who is chosen as role models and for what reason.

Case Study

Mole Models

Several government agencies allow their elected officials to have staff members who serve as policy advisers. Periodically, these staff members leave the elected official's office and seek employment in the bureaucracy. This process has mixed results. In some cases, the staff member has gained important knowledge, skills, and abilities that are of value to the organization. However, in just as many cases, insufficiently qualified staff members are forced on the organization by pressure from elected officials.

At times, these political placements occur because term limits push the elected official and staff out of office, and the elected official wants to reward staff members by allowing them to retain employment. At other times, it is a strategy aimed at placing an official's own people in strategic positions within the bureaucracy to serve as that official's eyes and ears (moles), and/or to gain increased control over the organization. In the latter case, staff members have inappropriately chosen their elected officials as role models and agreed to carry out their dubious motives within the bureaucracy.

It is important to bear in mind that this type of action violates both the spirit and the letter of the law, which calls for a veil of separation between elected officials who make policy decisions as a collective body (not as individuals) and administrators who are appointed to run the bureaucracy without undue interference from individual board members.

When illegitimate, politically motivated appointments are allowed, the system begins to break down. Former staff members of elected officials take their sense of entitlement and protection into the bureaucracy to do the sole bidding of one elected official, piercing the requirement of majority rule.

As this practice becomes more prevalent, these former staff members ignore the directives of their current supervisors and do the bidding of the elected officials who ultimately hire or fire the CEO. As this approach becomes institutionalized, it unfortunately creates a new path for success: start one's career as a staff member of an elected official, and even with limited credentials, one can be given a high-level, high-paying management position if one lets it be known that one is ready, willing, and able to do their bidding within the bureaucracy. The proliferation of this practice eventually destroys accountability within the organization and leads to the uncoordinated pursuit of singular agendas that eventually divide and conquer the organization from within.

Difficulty Transitioning into Management

The struggle of a line employee transitioning into a management position because of personal and/or organizational deficiencies.

Healthy and Normal Function

Candidates for first-level management positions should have a reasonable level of experience and an obvious aptitude for leading and coaching others. Those considered for promotion off the production floor should know and understand the new role they are considering, and make a commitment to learn new tasks rather than fall back on their former skill sets. The organization should endeavor to make this a win, as it can result in tremendous pride for the entire unit if one of their former coworkers succeeds.

The organization needs to be realistic regarding the abilities of its managerial candidates based upon a careful review of resumes and interviews. Additionally, the organization needs to recognize that it is almost certain that an individual who was once "one of the boys" will have difficulty initiating discipline or terminating former peers. As such, the organization should be very cautious about placing an insider in a management position over his or her former work unit with the expectation of improving efficiencies by cutting positions or demanding more discipline and productivity.

Causes of Dysfunction

- promoting managers not for their management ability but because they were top producers in a line job
- insufficient training for newly hired managers
- new managers who do not want to lose their hard-earned status as a top producer so they compete with their own staff instead of facilitating the staff's success
- difficulty of new managers in supervising, disciplining, reassigning, demoting, or firing people they used to work and be friends with

Risk to the Organization

The risk is that the new manager will revert back to his or her comfort level by performing line work and neglecting necessary management tasks like training, budgeting, scheduling, and performance management. An additional risk is that the former line worker will not be able to make the transition to effectively supervise and hold accountable former coworkers.

Symptoms and Signs

- new manager has difficulty understanding why all employees can't perform at a high level without assistance
- blank or confused look on the new manager's face from not knowing where to begin in the new job
- new manager neglects budgeting, scheduling, performance management, or other managerial duties
- new manager resisting impulse to go to the shop floor to fix the problem personally

Diagnostic Analysis

- Does the new manager consistently avoid necessary supervisory confrontations with former coworkers?
- Does the organization lack a training program for new managers?
- Are basic management tasks consistently performed in a quality or timely manner, or does the new manager seek to avoid them?
- Has there been a marked decline in production because of logistical issues not being addressed?
- Is there increasing tension between management and staff?

Progression and Impact

To minimize the impact of this disease, an organization must realize that being an executive chef does not necessarily train one to be a capable restaurateur. The skills are completely different. However, if the fragile assumption that a good x will develop into a good y is a continuing recruitment practice of the organization, the odds favor the kitchen over the business. The organization stands a good chance of losing twice, as the humiliating action of removing one's new general manager may cause that employee to not to want to serve in his or her former role and therefore leave the organization.

Prognosis

When a worker transitions into management, that individual should be dutifully monitored and assisted to ensure that the new duties are readily understood and adequately performed. If the new manager is a fish out of water, and training is either not made available or is not working, then the prognosis is poor. In a very short period of time, the previously productive unit will exhibit logistical strains and hiccups.

Treatment or Cure

- Require that those being hired for a first-time management position possess the necessary résumé or have demonstrated an aptitude for supervising employees.
- Have frank discussions about the requirements of management to determine whether training will be necessary. Encourage new managers to ask for help when needed.
- If possible, assign a mentor to the new manager.
- If you must remove the new manager, do it sooner rather than later, and work to have it be the new manager's idea, based on personal recognition that he or she is not cutting it.

Case Study

Not Ready for Prime Time

Al was a top producer at the shop level when he applied for a management job. Although Al's background demonstrated very little interest in or aptitude for leading others, the organization was thrilled to have the opportunity to promote one of their own. Since no one bothered to look at Al's resume, and senior management assumed that being an excellent technician would translate into being a good manager, no training was provided. Unfortunately, after fifteen months with Al in charge, the unit's quality and productivity had dropped by 50 percent, prompting senior management to review the situation.

In discussions with Al, senior management learned that the only reason Al took the position was because he figured he could do the same job and get a pay raise. Al revealed that he had no interest in managing and had never been asked whether he wanted or had the ability to mentor, train, or manage staff. Al was returned to his former position but with no pay reduction.

Lack of Creativity

A lack of ingenuity, originality, or resourcefulness applied to work issues.

Healthy and Normal Function

From top to bottom, an organization seeks to attract employees with motivation, creative zeal, and commitment. Those at the top should be organizational cheerleaders, with vision that provides direction, while those at the mid to lower levels are the creative talent who translate ideas into products and services that meet the needs of the customers. Leadership has a consistent pulse on the morale and development of product and service improvements to identify and address productivity lulls at the early stages.

Causes of Dysfunction

- lack of a comprehensive knowledge of the subject matter
- lack of initiative
- lack of confidence
- limited perspective
- boredom with the subject matter

Risk to the Organization

Employees with a general lack of creativity is a harbinger of a boring organization that lacks the vitality to attract and retain customers and quality employees. If those at the top are not creative and fail to hire people who are, the environment will be lackluster and one of general malaise.

Symptoms and Signs

- lack of vitality in the office
- clock-watching
- everything done by a rote process
- shortage of fresh, new ideas
- difficulty in getting people to work extra hours
- lack of camaraderie among leadership and staff

- absence of uniqueness in employees and activities
- need for personality transplants

Diagnostic Analysis

- Has there been a consistent exodus of the most creative staff members?
- Is there a lack of periodic product upgrades, process improvements, or customer service improvements?
- Is it difficult to get volunteers for new or unique projects?

Progression and Impact

Creativity is the lifeblood of an organization. In its absence, the organization is like a baseball player in a hitting slump. During the slump, the baseball looks as small as a peanut; the more effort the batter puts into the swing, the worse the results. Effort without results causes frustration and a loss of confidence. A loss of confidence lowers motivation, which eventually produces inactivity. Without creativity, the organization loses what makes it unique to the market and lessens its ability to provide a quality service or product.

Prognosis

Generally, the prognosis is good, as creative slumps come and go. However, if the slump is caused by a lack or absence of talent, the prognosis is bleak, and the organization's death can be slow and depressing.

Treatment or Cure

- Recruit for creativity in specific positions like product design, the idea/imagination department, and customer service.
- Ensure adequate time off for one's most creative staff members so they can recharge their batteries.
- Ensure leadership with vision and vitality.
- Provide offsite training or conferences to keep staff up-to-date on industry developments.
- Always have a place in the organization for those with plenty of constructive imagination.

Case Study

Where I Hang My Hat

A successful organization's recruiting staff was housed in the basement of an older building. Their office space was dark and dank, with closed offices arranged in long rows against the walls with very little common space. The furniture was old and odd-shaped for the offices. The office equipment was outdated, and it was difficult to get consistent Internet reception.

After a few years of interviewing disappointing applicants from company recruitments, management decided to hire a consultant to look into the problem. Before coming out to the workplace, the consultant reviewed recruitment documents to get a feel for the company's recruiting process. The recruitment bulletins and advertisements contained the necessary information, but the presentation was dull, repetitive, had an occasional typo, and included less than appealing photos.

Once the consultant came to the work site, the problem was obvious. An organization's physical office space, layout, decorations, furniture, and available equipment and tools have a far greater impact on creativity and culture than many people realize. If employees who were hired to bring creativity into the workforce and/or project a positive image are provided with poor working conditions, it will impact their morale and productivity.

In response to the consultant's findings, the company provided a better designed, more accommodating work space for its recruiting staff. Within a few months, the quality of work product and applicants (even for recruiter positions) increased tremendously.

Lack of Training

Staff's inability to efficiently and effectively accomplish the organization's mission and goals due to an inadequate level of training.

Healthy and Normal Function

The organization identifies the requirements of each job and determines whether customized training can be provided to increase efficiency and effectiveness—and thus, the company's return on investment. Training programs are designed to increase the accomplishment of the organization's mission and goals, and they are coordinated to ensure that the right people receive the right training at the right time and in the same manner for consistency. The organization maintains its cohesiveness by rotating its best managers among several key positions to gain an organization-wide focus.

Causes of Dysfunction

- leader's belief, based on personal experience and individual initiative to self-train, that customized training is not necessary
- high cost of providing training
- concern that training takes employees away from work
- difficulty finding customized training
- lack of knowledge of what training is available

Risk to the Organization

The risk to the organization is that staff members will be left to their own devices to acquire or improve necessary skills and abilities for their assignment. Without standardized training, employees may learn and practice their assignments in an inconsistent manner across the organization.

Symptoms and Signs

- large variance in productivity and inconsistent skill sets between employees performing the same job
- high rate of failure in a particular assignment

- frequent customer complaints
- poor supervisory practices because of a lack of training
- lack of cohesiveness and common practices between divisions of the company

Diagnostic Analysis

- Are a consistent number of costly mistakes being made by staff in performing their work?
- Do staff members consistently request training?
- Are customer complaints legitimate?
- How robust is the organization's training portfolio?
- Are inconsistent administrative practices utilized within the company?

Progression and Impact

In many organizations, when budget resources are scarce, one of the first things to go is training. When this occurs, the organizational "batting average" decreases because of employees having to learn their assignment on their own, rather than from those with the most success. In addition, the organization begins to fragment across organizational boundaries, losing its sense of a common identity, and inconsistently applying administrative policies and procedures.

An inadequately trained staff also lowers the productivity of an organization and increases the frustration level of both managers and workers. If left unaddressed, there are several critical organizational deficiencies that occur:

- high turnover rate because of a lack of corrective training
- lower return on investment
- inability to develop an effective succession planning program for the replacement of key staff
- utilization of multiple inconsistent approaches to the same work
- lack of customer confidence and a corresponding loss of business
- development of poor supervisor/subordinate relationships because of ill-trained supervisors

Over time, an organization that has a piecemeal approach to training leaves the success of the organization to chance and limps along based solely on its ability to consistently hire and retain quality staff.

Prognosis

If a robust training function is not present, over time the organization may lose its ability to efficiently and effectively achieve its mission and goals, and it may be unprepared to replace key executives.

Treatment or Cure

- Establish and reinforce training as one of the organization's key functions.
- Ensure the training group stays abreast of best-in-class training opportunities that are directly relevant to the organization.
- Conduct employee surveys to gauge training needs and the quality of training currently provided.
- Identify high-turnover jobs and determine if there is a training issue.
- Rotate managers with high potential among various assignments to gain a comprehensive understanding of the organization.

Case Study

The Training Has Left the Station

During the Great Recession, a large company survived by cutting several of its functions that were not directly related to the provision of goods and services. One of the cuts was to the central training program. Each organizational unit took over responsibility for its own training needs. As a result, training became piecemeal throughout the organization, with critical training in areas like supervisory skills and performance management falling by the wayside.

In this environment, each division trained employees in its own way. In a company with more than twenty separate divisions, each division became a silo, making it difficult to coordinate and provide consistency across the organization. In addition, it was difficult for the organization to have any kind of quality succession program for executive jobs, as employees became less and less transitional between divisions, curtailing the C-suite's ability to get to know many of the executives in different roles.

Eventually, when economic times improved, the company benefited greatly from centralizing generic training functions across the organization, which provided bridges for cooperation and consistent skill development. As a result, improvements were noted in the following areas: supervisory management, business writing, leadership development, more comprehensive and easily understood policies and procedures, and the emotional intelligence of the staff.

Looting of Staff

The reallocating of staff resources from a successful organizational unit to a poor performing unit without fixing the root cause of the problem.

Healthy and Normal Function

The root cause(s) of poorly performing organizational units is identified and addressed. High performers assist in the process as necessary but not as a go-to strategy. In cases where high performers are needed on a temporary basis, all are rewarded for their contributions.

Causes of Dysfunction

- belief that the poorly performing unit has to survive
- belief that the poorly performing unit can be turned around by the temporary reallocation of staff
- belief that the well-run unit will always be well run and can therefore afford to loan some of its best staff out

Risk to the Organization

The risks are that a well-functioning unit will be weakened by losing quality staff, and that their reallocation will not make a sufficient difference in solving the identified problem.

Symptoms and Signs

- managers looking for a quick fix
- unconfirmed assumptions about the reasons for the problems associated with the poorly run unit
- employees transferred to the poorly run unit unhappy about the move
- poorly run unit continues to experience the same problems after six months

Diagnostic Analysis

- Is there a consistent movement of good employees to units experiencing problems?
- Are both units experiencing difficulties after the move?

- Has the root cause(s) of the unit's poor performance been identified?
- Has there been little or no progress made in improving the poorly operating unit?

Progression and Impact

This disease typically does not progress very far in an organization because of its low rate of success. In most cases, it doesn't sufficiently improve the organization and frustrates the good employees who were moved to help out.

However, if the company chooses to utilize this approach on a consistent basis, it can have debilitating results. Once implemented, there will be a hesitancy to undo the personnel moves, thereby causing extended periods of distress in the organization. This approach can cause a high level of dissatisfaction among a company's best employees and also within the poorly performing units, which are embarrassed at being designated as underperformers.

Prognosis

This disease usually heals itself as leadership fails to see a sufficient return on investment to continue its use. However, if multiple moves are made and linger without sufficient improvements, the prognosis is continuing discontent among the best performers.

Treatment or Cure

- Only try this approach in extreme situations in which immediate relief is needed to stop the bleeding in a poorly performing unit.
- Make a commitment to move good employees out of the unit anytime they request it.
- Identify the root cause of the poor performance and directly address those issues before moving good employees to the underperforming unit.

Case Study

A Heist Gone Bad

An organization decided to centralize its IT function in an effort to increase the effective and efficient management of a critical cost center. In order to increase the chances of success, many of the best IT and administrative personnel were transferred to the central IT group to plan, coordinate, and implement the necessary changes.

One effect of transferring staff was to significantly weaken IT operations in the organizational units they left. In addition, the centralization effort took much longer than anticipated, leaving the depleted organizational units floundering for a considerable period of time. More concerning was that even after the movement of personnel, several of the critical organization-wide IT problems did not improve because they were political issues created by the board of directors, which the consolidation of talent into the central IT group had no impact on.

As a result, the "temporary" looting of IT staff was overextended and did very little to help either the individual organization units or centralized efforts.

Selecting Unqualified Leaders

The placement of less-than-qualified employees into positions of leadership because promotions are not based on merit but are strategic moves to secure and elevate organizational position and perks.

Healthy and Normal Function

An organization's most important resource is its employees. As such, employees should be guided by leaders who have the organization's best interests at heart, not merely their own. Individual roles and responsibilities must be developed for each position, along with a breakdown of the education, experience, and ethical attributes needed to fill each position. Hires should be based on merit. When performance issues occur, the organization identifies and evaluates the specific leadership deficiencies and knows when "making a repair" is the most appropriate action or when "changing parts" is the right course of action.

Causes of Dysfunction

- effort to retain power by promoting and thereby purchasing loyalty from those who could not reach the top based upon their skills or ensuring that no one who could replace the leader is promoted into critical positions
- selections made by those who are not adequately qualified to assess talent and/or are using poor selection criteria
- effort to satisfy the ego and homogenize the organization by hiring employees who are like the leader so that the leader only sees a reflection of his or her personality
- acquiescing to political pressure to promote certain individuals in return for a higher position and/or pay

Risk to the Organization

The risk to the organization of contracting this disease increases with the promotion of each less-than-qualified person. This is particularly true if those promoted possess or demonstrate personality disorders like antisocial, avoidant, borderline, obsessive-compulsive, narcissistic, or schizotypal.[11] This happens more frequently than one might expect, given that their willing acceptance of unwarranted positions of authority is oftentimes a byproduct of these disorders.

---

[11] American Psychiatric Association, *Diagnostic and Statistical Manual of Mental Disorders,* 5th ed. (Arlington, VA: American Psychiatric Publishing, 2013).

The risks to the organization of placing the wrong people in the wrong positions are enormous. Unqualified people produce lower quality work and typically make less satisfactory choices and selections themselves. If illegitimate promotions spread, the organization becomes bastardized and cannot compete in the workplace, eventually succumbing to its self-inflicted propagation deficiencies.

Symptoms and Signs

- manipulations of the hiring process, such as employees promoted to the C-suite from the middle of the organization, skipping over promotional levels without developing the requisite skills
- those promoted with insufficient experience irresponsibly diving in as if they know exactly what to do, making their introductions with a belly flop off the high dive
- obnoxious attitude of those promoted who were born on third base but think they hit a triple
- Group Think decisions where everyone agrees with the most powerful or influential person in the room
- implementation of pragmatic rather than ethical choices
- unqualified leaders giving verbal and vague output rather than precise and penciled
- lack of spontaneity or random outpouring of fun in the workplace
- best, brightest, most ethical leaders ignored and maligned, increasingly becoming frustrated and considering a departure from the organization
- significant issues allowed to linger that cause unnecessary damage to the organization
- inner circle or clique of the insufficiently qualified becoming the new "disaster race" for the organization

Diagnostic Analysis

- Is there a proliferation of dichotomous situations: wrong becomes right, inexperience is more valued than experience, the less qualified get paid more than the qualified, people are publicly praised who achieved success through dubious means, and the ethically challenged are given more latitude and extra organizational lives?
- Is the leader unable to perform the essential functions of the job?
- On reviewing résumés, are those promoted insufficiently qualified for their positions?
- What does the hiring authority have to say about why these employees were hired?
- Are illogical and death-defying organizational feats attempted without a safety net?

- Do the inexperienced replicate themselves in cascading waves from the top to the bottom of the organization?
- Is there a lack of quality communication coming out of the C-suite?
- Have ill-thought-out decisions ultimately failed?

Progression and Impact

This is a traveling disease with a passport. The progression and impact of the disease to the organization is largely dependent upon how many unqualified people are hired, the criticality of the positions they occupy, and whether these hires are random or coordinated acts aimed at taking over control of an organization. Of course, with every poor choice made, the more negative the impact. Whacked people tend to hire other whacked people.

This disease also increases the access of "the great unqualified" to multiple touchpoints in the organization, thus providing more outlets for deficiencies to spread and mutate. The worst possible scenario is that the governing body itself orchestrates the establishment of the mediocracy. As part of this takeover process, the loyally incompetent are strategically placed to assist in concealing information, limiting dissent, and manipulating consensus—all to reduce any chance for the unqualified leaders' early demise.

Each organization's tipping point for achieving mediocrity is different, depending upon how many bad hires have to occur before the organization changes its status from a critical to a hospice condition. Since the goal of those orchestrating the takeover is to keep the organization running so that they can continue to rule their fiefdom, executives must retain just enough talented people in critical positions to assure sustainability. However, in the end, this game can't be won. It always results in a house divided against itself that eventually crumbles.

Another insidious outcome of this disease is the impact it has on the organization's intelligent, qualified, and ethical employees. The further the disease progresses, the more the organization's best and brightest are subjected to being ruled by their inferiors. As an example, many times inexperienced leaders don't understand the significance of what they are being told by the seasoned professionals. To make matters worse, the inexperienced sometimes falsely believe they belong in their positions of authority and view the seasoned employees as the ones who don't get it. Unfortunately, their naiveté and inexperience paralyze their ability to make timely, tough decisions, and ultimately result in scorched-earth impacts to the organization from not dealing with critical deficiencies in a timely manner.

Prognosis

Nearly every organization has employees in positions of authority who should not be there. Minor damage occurs but is curable if the disease is isolated to less-important organizational functions. Catastrophic failure results if poor promotions are made at the top, and these poor choices replicate themselves down through the organization.

A healthy organization will have a robust evaluation system that quickly identifies these employees and either trains them to sufficiency or weeds them out. In these cases, the organization tends to bounce back rather quickly as the organization learns from its mistakes.

However, if the disease is left untreated, it metastasizes quickly. If the hiring of under-qualified leaders does not attack a vital organizational function, the mass may be isolated and treatable without long-term negative effects. However, if it spreads to several vital parts of the organization, it may become impossible to effectively combat and result in the demise of the organization.

Treatment or Cure

- Hire an experienced, competent, and ethical CEO who will set the appropriate tone for the organization.
- Don't make a habit of promoting people who skip organizational levels and miss critical developmental opportunities (just as you wouldn't allow a five-year-old to drive a car).
- Develop clear policies in the areas of recruitment and retention, performance evaluation, and discipline that call for all hires and continuing employment to be based on merit.
- Utilize evidence-based recruiting tools to ensure that applicants can demonstrate legitimate experience and education. Avoid anecdotal or generic background references about the perceived skill sets of individuals.
- Disciplinary action should be taken against those who violate these policies and quick decisions reached about those who continually exhibit an inability to measure up to their leadership assignment.
- In instances where an under-qualified leader is trainable and the assignment is not immediately detrimental to the organization, take the time to work with and train the individual into an acceptable level of performance.

Case Study

Trying to Get It Wrong

A citizen, Sonia, requested government assistance to address a private development issue. Sonia was assisted by a member of the governing board and that person's staff. After the request was satisfactorily addressed, Sonia was interested in becoming an employee of the organization. Surprisingly, the governing member saw to it that a job offer was tendered, reporting to a high-level executive. However, when the Great Recession immediately followed, the offer was rescinded.

The member of the governing board was embarrassed, and his staff spent the next five years looking for a suitable job for Sonia. During this time, Sonia applied for dozens of random top-level jobs in the organization that no one person could possibly be qualified to fill. One position was for a manager at a remote public facility. Sonia did not meet the minimum qualifications for the job and was appropriately screened out early in the recruitment. However, a couple of years later, a temporary need to fill this position became available. Fortuitously for Sonia, the job happened to be in an area that was now supervised by a former staff member of the governing board member who had originally assisted her.

Before she was offered the temporary position, Sonia was asked to meet with peer managers to get their input. To a person, the peers did not want a job offer to be tendered to Sonia. Their concerns were dismissed, and Sonia was hired—even though she had previously applied for this job and was screened out early in the process for failing to meet minimum standards. Shortly thereafter, the person who hired Sonia was promoted to a higher position within the organization. To Sonia's chagrin, the supervisor's replacement was one of the peers who had originally recommended against hiring her. To no one's surprise, Sonia was eventually released from the temporary assignment and another candidate was chosen for the permanent job.

Sonia spent the next few years filing complaints claiming that the person selected for the permanent position was chosen because of various discrimination issues. For years, Sonia harangued the entity at all levels with her complaints, constantly demanding redress. No discipline was ever administered against the managers or former staff members of the governing body who for five years violated the government entity's recruitment rules by proactively searching for a job for a person who was not qualified.

Unaccountable Leaders

The refusal or reluctance to hold leadership accountable for misdeeds and/or performance deficiencies.

Healthy and Normal Function

The organization requires that all its employees accept responsibility for their actions and perform at a satisfactory level in return for their pay. Employees learn from their mistakes and take the steps necessary to remedy deficiencies. The organization appropriately addresses those who refuse to accept responsibility or perform at a satisfactory level.

Causes of Dysfunction

- no legitimate organizational mechanism to objectively assess and respond to significant allegations of corruption or poor performance by those in the highest positions of authority
- leaders hired and retained based on loyalty and exempted from everyday accountability
- initiation pledge taken by those at the top declaring that they are immune from accountability and committed to protecting each other
- pragmatic decision not to rock the luxury boat that pays the bills
- retribution and retaliation against whistleblowers

Risk to the Organization

The risk to an organization of not holding leaders accountable for misdeeds or poor performance are substantial. Impacts include not addressing the root cause of problems, communicating to employees that the rule of policy does not apply to those in power, and a potential increase of organizational vigilantism to resolve issues.

Symptoms and Signs

- unresolved personnel issues that never seem to get fixed
- public airing (leaks) of organization misdeeds because they are not handled internally
- employees no longer bringing problems to leadership
- midlevel managers establishing their own working groups to address unresolved issues

- leaders never apologize or see any reason to change
- apparent double standards
- a practice of false pacification of legitimate complainants by telling them they are absolutely right and promising that their issues will be addressed

Diagnostic Analysis

- Is it well known and communicated among the workforce that promotions and hiring decisions are not based on merit?
- Does a review of lawsuits or complaints show that no legitimate investigations were conducted and no action was taken against the guilty?
- Were retaliatory actions taken against legitimate complainants, including attempts to find or falsely manufacture "dirt" on the complainant or the complainant being passed over for pay raises and promotions?
- Does leadership appear to have an entitlement mentality?
- Do leaders receive and accept any training?
- Have leaders ever have any suggestions for improvement in their performance reviews?

Progression and Impact

Lack of accountability is a disease created by and for leadership. The disease has its onset the first time an executive feels that reaching the top equates to certain perks and organizational exemptions. One exemption is from performance evaluation and accountability. Those at the top usually look after each other. Once this disease is formalized as a perk, it spreads contagiously throughout the executive ranks. Eventually, everyone has the disease, and so it appears as if no one has the disease.

Complainants are routinely dismissed as jealous and retaliatory, angry that they have not risen into the executive ranks. The more valuable employees/complainants are initially engaged to see if they can be persuaded to look the other way, since they have a skill set important to the employer. Others are dared to litigate at their own financial and reputational risk. Typically, this perk is not allowed to spread down to middle and lower levels of the organization because someone has to do the work and be held accountable for the organization to survive.

Once someone who tests positive for unaccountability is allowed to remain in a position of leadership, the disease takes hold. If it is acknowledged that the person had to be hired because of who they know, the disease can be quarantined. However, if the unaccountable person is allowed to spread the contagion by hiring his or her own people or gains more influence across the organization, the disease will spread rapidly.

A controlling factor in the spread of the disease is whether lack of accountability is seen as a gift or a perk. If it is seen as a gift, it is up to the organization to determine who will be granted unaccountability. If it is a perk, then it is automatically granted upon entrance into upper management. If it is a gift, controls can be placed on how it spreads; if it is a perk, there is no control, the mutation begins, and proliferation is inevitable.

Toward the end, scandals occur that may be large enough to sink the organization. The sad facts are exposed, other abuses become known, and the company's reputation is severely damaged. The scandal is typically a case that is innocently damning or one in which an executive breaks ranks and confirms the inside story.

Prognosis

The impact to the organization is entirely dependent on the response of its governing body and CEO. If the organization has a legitimate mechanism in place whereby its employees can go for an honest fix, and if leadership keeps accountability waivers to a minimum, the organization can regenerate itself after a minor illness. However, if unaccountability is a club that can be joined by paying the appropriate dues (loyalty, lineage, looking the other way, buying in), the disorder will spread and contaminate the organization until it is severe enough that it has to be addressed.

Treatment or Cure

- Establish and maintain a clear system of accountability that includes publication of organizational values and standards, training of those standards provided to employees, and a legitimate organizational mechanism to investigate and adjudicate complaints.
- Don't ignore; intervene.
- Require unaccountable persons to fix the problems they create.
- Transfer have-to-retain unaccountable persons to the least impactful part of the organization.
- Do reference checks to hire skilled and psychologically healthy employees.

Case Study

Turning Both Cheeks

Barbara was the CEO of an organization who was committed to ensuring that those gratuitously placed in positions of power by the board of directors would remain there at any cost. Whenever examples of abuse perpetrated by those political appointments were submitted, there would nearly always be an effort to slow down, deflect attention, or drop the complaint. Examples of statements made by Barbara during her cover-up attempts include:

- "We already looked into the issue. Nothing is there."
- "I hired an outside investigator. I ensured that they didn't find anything. I mean, I assured that they looked at everything but didn't find anything."
- "We shouldn't keep records on personal comings and goings. It just muddies the waters."
- "Let's have someone else look into this. We have other more important things to focus on."
- "You already have some members of the board of directors who don't like you. Do you want more of them to not like you if you continue to push this agenda?"
- "Why do you have to bring all this negative stuff up? You're supposed to make my life easier."
- "I've paid my special counsel to look at this, and they said the recommendations for discipline were too harsh."
- "You just don't have the proper perspective on this."
- "I guess we just have a different perspective on conflicts of interests, contract manipulation, recruitment violations, favoritism, claims of noncompliance, and dishonesty. My perspective pays more."

Chapter 9

Process Deficiencies

The Runaround

- Lack of Analytics
- Lack of Customer Focus
- Ineffective/Inefficient Update of Internal Controls
- Regulatory and Compliance Inefficiency

Lack of Analytics

A lack of key performance indicators to ascertain how well the organization is achieving its mission and goals.

Healthy and Normal Function

The organization assigns staff to identify, develop, and track clear performance measures that capture and gauge the quality and amount of productivity of the operation.

Causes of Dysfunction

- concern with the time and money required to develop a robust analytical function
- fear of what the results might show

Risk to the Organization

The risks to the organization of having insufficient analytical data is that the organization may have no idea how well or poorly it is performing, or, if the organization is not achieving the degree of success desired, it will be difficult to ascertain the reasons for this, or know what adjustments need to be made.

Symptoms and Signs

- lack of key performance measures
- solutions to problems based on intuition or conjecture
- difficulty in holding employees accountable due to a lack of verifiable data

Diagnostic Analysis

- How do employees know they have achieved the goals or objectives of the organization?
- How does management ascertain who are the top performers?
- How does management know if the organization is operating effectively and efficiently?

Progression and Impact

If an organization fails to establish a meaningful analytics capability, it will be difficult to know just how well or poorly the organization is doing. In many ways, the organization will be operating in the dark, without adequate information to make informed decisions about resource allocation, employee performance, and whether it should contract or expand its operation and in what areas. In such an environment, easy fixes are missed because they are not identified, and early warning signs of critical deficiencies are not noted until it is too little, too late. In addition, it will be difficult to know how to reward or address employee deficiencies absent specific criteria and measurements.

Prognosis

If meaningful analytics are not established, it will be like a pilot flying blind without instrumentation to document speed, direction, altitude, or local terrain. This situation may be fine if the weather is good and visibility is clear, but when the weather's stormy, it's a crapshoot. An organization that is directionally in the dark can only hope for the best when it encounters conditions that present unknown obstacles. Management won't see the mountain obscured by the clouds until it is too late to bank or ascend.

Treatment or Cure

- Establish clear metrics that measure the productivity and quality of the unit from the customer's perspective.
- Hire an analytics manager or consultant to develop, track, and report on metrics.
- Do something with the data: be transparent and release it to staff, use it to make necessary organizational changes, or use it for performance management.

Case Study

Ignorance Is Blistering

An organization's central purchasing department was responsible for processing a high volume and variety of purchasing requests, including commodities, professional services, equipment, and construction design and build projects. In providing this internal service, the purchasing department did not have any performance measures to gauge customer satisfaction regarding their level of productivity or quality of service. The procurements were processed in a FIFO manner (first in, first out) with no ability or interest in handling rush orders. Furthermore, management did not track the amount of time it took to place an order or the hours expended by staff on any specific order or type of purchase.

Without this basic information, the department was unable to operate in an effective and efficient manner and received consistent complaints from its clients. In addition, without objective information, the purchasing department was free to make up or exaggerate workload or make other mysterious claims as a rationale for poor performance. Ultimately, the problem became so pronounced that executive management was forced to address these bottlenecks by replacing the manager and establishing performance measures to ensure ongoing effectiveness.

Lack of Customer Focus

Customer satisfaction is not driving a company's product/service offerings, and customer opinions are often viewed as burdensome, unwelcome, or something to avoid.

Healthy and Normal Function

The organization establishes performance measures that are driven by the needs of the customer. Employees are able to identify specific activities that directly support customer needs. They understand that a significant part of their rewards structure will be based on their ability to provide quality customer service on a consistent basis.

Causes of Dysfunction

- an attitude that the organization knows best what the customer needs and wants
- a strategy to marginally meet the needs of its customers, finding the precise tipping point at which a majority will continue to purchase the company's products and services
- monopolistic control over the provision of goods and services
- technical or resource considerations that limit what can be made available to the customer

Risk to the Organization

If a company cannot meet the needs of its customers, those customers will go elsewhere. If they are unable to go elsewhere, customers may feel so frustrated that they will unite in their demands for new company leadership.

Symptoms and Signs

- no effective way to meaningfully survey customer satisfaction, or worse, no desire for such information
- product or service offerings driven by corporate, not customer, preference
- noticeable deterioration in service quality
- intense frustration and palpable anger demonstrated by customers over lack of quality service

Diagnostic Analysis

- Is there an intentional lack of an established mechanism to accept customer complaints, or is the mechanism used so frustrating that most customers just give up?
- Does company policy require that all complaints or claims be initially denied and only reconsidered if the customer makes a substantial fuss?
- How does organizational leadership know whether or not the customer is pleased with the goods or services provided?
- What are the results of observing the quality of goods/services during site inspections or by purposefully becoming one of the organization's customers?
- When surveyed immediately after interfacing with the organization, what do customers have to say?

Progression and Impact

The impact of this disease in a for-profit environment is typically quick and painful. If there are other competitors in the marketplace, customers will rapidly gravitate to the best product or service for the price. If an organization makes it clear that customer needs cannot be met, they clearly make a statement that they don't want the customer's business.

The progression of this disease in either a government entity or private enterprise that has a monopoly can be quite different, as customers have fewer options. We say "fewer" rather than "no" options to make an important distinction. When customers have nowhere else to go for a particular good or service, it may take quite a number of bad experiences to get them to react; however, if they are repeatedly ignored or abused, this may trigger a visceral response. Having nowhere else to go places people in a corner. If the service they need is imperative, providing a legitimate reason to lash out will make them a powerful force.

Prognosis

If the organization can make a reasonable effort to address complaints, particularly for those who have been wronged, it will be able to minimize its loss of customers. However, if the organization takes advantage of those who have nowhere else to go, they risk a coordinated groundswell of negative reaction that may go public. Once the disregard for the customer becomes endemic, the situation can only be remedied by a change in management or by voting out elected officials. If this occurs, it will take years for the entity to rebuild the trust and loyalty of its clientele.

Treatment or Cure

- Pursue early intervention with a change in focus that makes legitimate customer needs a priority. This can be accomplished by formal training for employees and the solicitation of customer input on a regular and confidential basis.
- If the entity has grown contemptuous of the customer, nothing short of new leadership with major attitudinal and operational changes will be able to replace an employee convenience focus with a customer convenience focus.

Case Study

This Is Not My First Road-eo

Construction efforts to widen a certain city road had been blocking traffic for over a year, yet it appeared as if little progress had been made. Finally, a city councilman became fed up with constituent complaints regarding the delays and investigated the situation with his public works manager. Initially, the manager simply dismissed the councilman's frustration with flippant retorts like, "Rome wasn't built in a day." Prompted by the lack of a definitive response, the councilman established a task force to investigate the reason for the project delays.

It was discovered that the councilman's concerns were entirely correct, as almost no progress had been made on the project in over a year. The manager was stringing out the project as long as possible so that union members would continue to have a local job and not have to move on to the next assignment, which required long-distance travel. This fact was well known within the public works department and had been the driving force in all major roadwork projects.

Following this discovery, the city manager disciplined the public works manager and ensured that this practice was no longer utilized. The road project was completed shortly thereafter, to the relief of the public.

▬ Ineffective/Inefficient Update of Internal Controls ▬

Leadership is cemented to its outdated control mechanisms and fails to appreciate how ineffective internal controls can stifle productivity and morale.

Healthy and Normal Function

Internal processes are periodically updated based on input from company staff and customers. All employees responsible for processing transactions fully understand the entire process, each person's role in the process, and how each step adds value.

Causes of Dysfunction

- leaders who are out of touch with internal processes and procedures
- leaders who have not assessed processes and procedures for some time and continue to enforce old and counterproductive methods
- leaders who don't know how to design effective/efficient internal control processes

Risk to the Organization

The risk is that antiquated internal processes will cause ineffective/inefficient use of resources and keep the organization from delivering quality and timely services to its customers.

Symptoms and Signs

- bottlenecks and time delays in processing
- customers who have created alternatives to the established process to get better and quicker service
- staff members who break internal controls outright or invent reasons for not following the rules in order to avoid bottlenecks
- frustrated processing staff who are stuck utilizing ineffective/inefficient processes that add little value and result in customer criticism

Diagnostic Analysis

- Are there complaints from both internal and external customers about slow response times?
- Have cumbersome and counterproductive processes led to poor morale and low productivity among the staff?
- Has there been an exodus of talented staff from the processing group because of frustration?
- Are deviations from established processes increasing?

Progression and Impact

The progression of this disease depends on whether the organization takes steps to ensure that the processes work for the company rather than the company working for the processes. The latter condition is typically the result of either leadership neglect or lack of experience. Either leadership doesn't want to invest the time to fix the situation (neglect to protect), or doesn't know how to fix the problem (the curse of making things worse).

Prognosis

A choice arises to either continue with the menu or update it. Updating internal control processes will eventually heal the disease. Continuing with the menu means feeding the same old slop to one's workers and customers, which ultimately results in long-term negative consequences.

Treatment or Cure

- Institute a 360-degree survey of internal and external customers on a periodic basis to measure the quality, usefulness, timeliness, and value of established policies and procedures and their associated processes.
- Consider practicing a zero-based imaginary process flow with staff and customers in order to identify the must-have steps, checks, and balances the majority thinks are beneficial. Discard the old processes.
- Consult with professional associations for best practices.
- Require management to periodically walk through these processes from cradle to grave to personally assess the value of the processes and identify choke points and redundancies.
- Reward staff for identifying better ways of doing things.

Case Study

The More the Unmerrier

A large multibillion-dollar entity never flow-charted its outdated process for property acquisition. Instead, the company relied upon a decades-old process that required seven different organizational units' involvement and approval. Predictably, the process was slow and subject to reversals and delays from paperwork getting lost in the shuffle between units and personnel. Not surprisingly, even after all unit approvals were received, there were times when a manager would suggest that a step in the process was skipped. Sometimes this approach of pointing to a flawed system was used as a basis for stopping a property acquisition a manager didn't agree with.

Upon internal review, auditors discovered that out of the seven required approvals, only the first one really mattered or added any value. Interviews revealed that the last six approvers had no idea why the transaction was being routed to them, as they did not actually review or challenge the transaction in any way. As a result, over decades, the organization made little progress in accomplishing its real estate transactions.

Regulatory and Compliance Inefficiency

Ineffectively and inefficiently promulgating and complying with government regulatory schemes.

Healthy and Normal Function

Government and industry come together to identify and solve a commonly understood problem. Both sides partner to properly address the public concern and effectively achieve the aims of their respective organizations. Politics are minimized in the process.

Causes of Dysfunction

On the regulatory side:

- legislators and/or regulators whose primary goal is to make a political statement rather than solve a problem
- promulgation of extreme (vague or overbearing) regulations and implementation of an unreasonable solution that is too wide of a pendulum swing from the current condition
- regulatory staff without the requisite experience to ascertain compliance
- regulatory staff with a personal philosophical bent that unreasonably controls industry activities
- inadequate number of staff to monitor and evaluate compliance in a timely manner

On the compliance side:

- organizations that respond to regulations in the extreme, either with substantial noncompliance or by overdoing their own internal policies and procedures
- organizations that assign their most inexperienced or least qualified staff to the management of regulatory issues

Risk to the Organization

An inefficient regulatory scheme and/or minimally qualified compliance staff negatively impacts an organization's ability to meet the needs of society in a particular area. As a result, organizations are forced to operate in a less efficient and effective manner that fails to either satisfactorily address the concerns that prompted the legislation or provide a timely service to its customers. When this occurs, the legislative and compliance cure can turn out to be worse than the disease.

On the organization side, there is a tendency at times to assign one's least qualified staff to work with regulators and on internal compliance activities. The subsequent risk to the organization is that ineffective and inefficient policies and procedures are developed that either under- or over-comply with regulations. In addition, having one's least qualified staff interact with regulators reduces opportunities for creative solutions between the parties.

Symptoms and Signs

- problems that, although identified, don't get solved in a timely manner, resulting in industry and public frustration
- excessive cost to comply with regulations, which negates an organization's ability to devote adequate resources to solving the problem
- charging organizations for the cost of complying with regulations they do not agree with
- complex and/or incoherent regulations
- legislation and accompanying regulations that are approved before sufficient review by impacted industries
- substantial conflict between regulators and the organization

Diagnostic Analysis

- Do regulators have total but less than competent control over an industry?
- Is the problem that created the legislation no longer a problem by the time the regulations are promulgated?
- Are businesses closing their doors because of the excessive cost of compliance?
- Do regulators fail to see the value of the legislation passed?
- Are there organizations that repeatedly fail to conform to regulations?
- Do organizations repeatedly use the same tactics to hide noncompliance from regulators?
- Has an organization's compliance staff lost touch with organizational goals and objectives, insisting instead on rigid perfectionism in its adherence to regulations, unnecessarily sacrificing company resources and thereby increasing customer costs?

Progression and Impact

This is a nasty disease because regulatory mandates are enforceable by law. Typically, enacting legislation requires a single acute or a series of chronic events that mobilize public opinion. Since there are many issues on the public agenda, it's only a matter of time before an issue is replaced by other concerns. As such, resources are typically marshaled quickly in an effort to slap together legislation to address the problem. In this hurried environment, it is difficult to craft a consensus on which subject-matter experts should be consulted to draft balanced legislation that efficiently and effectively solves the problem, is not overly burdensome, and can be reasonably implemented. During this process, it is critical not to overreact with an extreme fix that makes the cure worse than the disease. Once legislation is passed, draft regulations are issued that propose policies and procedures for implementing the legislation. This includes determining which regulatory agency will be responsible for monitoring compliance.

Such monitors are typically government workers or low-bid contractors working for the government. They acquire considerable power over an industry, as they determine whether or not companies are in compliance with the letter and intent of the legislation. In many cases, because of budgetary constraints, this is added workload to an already taxed staff. Thus, there may be insufficient time to adequately train monitors to understand the nuances of the industry or the issues being addressed. There may also be limited time to review and make determinations on regulatory approvals that would allow businesses to quickly move forward with projects. As a result, the industry can be held hostage by the under-qualified and understaffed, and proposed projects may not be sufficiently reviewed or completed in a timely manner or meet the needs of the public.

On the organizational side, companies who see regulatory compliance as a necessary evil tend to minimize attention in this area and/or assign their least qualified staff to manage this function. Over time, this approach results in less efficient and effective solutions to regulatory compliance. If inadequate attention is given to compliance, the company may find itself having poor relationships with regulators, being fined for noncompliance, or developing compliance activities that are excessive, overly burdensome, and costly.

Prognosis

The prognosis depends upon whether there is sufficient experience, foresight, or time to develop an effective and efficient legislative/regulatory/compliance scheme on both the government and organization levels that adequately addresses the issue at hand.

Treatment or Cure

- Allow ample time for both sides to understand the issue and its root causes.
- Ensure that the most qualified individuals representing the various concerns be assigned to develop a workable solution to the issue.
- Assign regulatory agency leadership with the necessary authority to ensure the proposed legislation and regulatory scheme is properly developed, without undue political influence.
- Assign sufficiently competent organizational staff to work on regulatory compliance issues.
- Develop balanced legislation and regulatory guidelines that best meet the needs of both sides and will be practical to implement.
- Ensure that regulatory staff assigned to monitor compliance are well trained and understand their role in ensuring compliance without introducing personal bias.

Case Study

Trash Is Cash

The most common method of dealing with a region's solid waste (trash) is to dispose of it in a landfill. Because of increased federal regulations, former "dumps" that could essentially just unload and cover up trash have now been transformed into solid waste facilities (sanitary landfills). Modern landfills are large and complicated construction sites that regulate the types of waste that can be buried and have numerous, costly systems for collecting landfill gas (e.g., methane), leachate (rain water that leaches through the buried trash), and carrying out the mandatory replacement of impacted habitat and protected species.

Most landfills operate within a specified geographic footprint that regulates daily tonnage received, with limitations on the final height and width of buried waste. In addition, most of today's landfills also host recycling activities, and some have energy production capabilities like converting landfill gas into electricity. On the financing side, many landfill operators have solid waste disposal agreements in place that guarantee a fixed dumping fee to customers in exchange for a guarantee from municipalities and trash haulers that all of the jurisdiction's trash will come to the regional landfill.

In such an environment, siting and permitting a new landfill is a monumental bureaucratic feat that can take as long as a decade from initiation to completion. There are multiple players involved: the public jurisdiction where the landfill will be sited, the regulators, citizen concerns, trash-hauler issues, landfill-operator issues, etc.

Once a landfill is opened, regulatory issues do not subside; in fact, they intensify. One would think that if a landfill operator could receive a permit to build a landfill—which is essentially governmental approval to build a trash mountain—that all other, less environmentally invasive, mandated site activities to run the facilitate would be included. Not so. Everything, and I mean *everything*, requires a permit, even the building of bathroom facilities. Some have even speculated that going to the bathroom might require a permit.

The effective and efficient implementation of a new landfill is largely dependent on the skill sets of all those involved in the process. If inexperienced staff are assigned to regulate, permit, and operate a new landfill, the project may never get off the ground—or if it does, it will be mired in excessive cost, time delays, and mind-bending operational process barriers. The inability to address a jurisdiction's solid waste needs is a public safety issue as well as a financial concern. The further the trash disposal site is from the jurisdiction, the more cost to the consumer.

Chapter 10

Resource Management Deficiencies

Slim Pickings

- Inadequate Resources
- Misdiagnosis

Inadequate Resources

The lack of sufficient resources (such as budget, personnel, and equipment) to satisfactorily accomplish an assignment.

Healthy and Normal Function

All levels of the organization understand and pursue the mission and goals of the organization in an optimal manner. Each employee understands his or her role in the process and that each person efficiently doing his or her part contributes to the sustainability of the organization. The organization adeptly establishes annual priorities and work plans based on what projects or services can be adequately funded and resourced. The organization avoids establishing overly aggressive work plans that cannot be properly resourced and will result in partially completed projects.

Causes of Dysfunction

- lack of sufficient funds to adequately complete a project
- lack of familiarity with operations to properly estimate the resources needed
- inadequate internal processes to ensure the timely delivery of resources
- resources of insufficient quality

Risk to the Organization

Organizations require sufficient and quality resources to optimize their efficiency and effectiveness. When not available, the organization improvises and typically underachieves, ultimately failing to meet its goals. In addition, these adjustments in many cases have negative domino effects throughout the organization.

Symptoms and Signs

- longer time required to accomplish tasks
- excessive downtime because of uncoordinated tasks
- need to reengineer project scopes, schedules, and budgets
- frustration, low morale, and lack of enthusiasm among employees
- decreased quality of service
- a constant need to fix quick fixes

Diagnostic Analysis

- Are projects regularly not completed on time?
- Are other projects completed in an inefficient and ineffective way, with expensive change orders and work-arounds?
- Are important projects consistently underfunded in the annual budget process?
- Do managers have little time to manage because they have to provide hands-on involvement to deal with inadequate resources?

Progression and Impact

Having insufficient resources is akin to not having the right tool to do a home repair. It makes the difference between a five-minute versus a five-hour fix. Organizations that chronically face this issue are at a severe disadvantage.

Organizational and project planning is typically done from the perspective of trying to accomplish the optimal result. As such, each task is planned around having the right resources, at the right time, performed by the right people. When resources are inadequate, not received on time, or performed by those with inadequate skill sets, the negative impacts cascade throughout the process. Each weak link complicates and expands the combinations and permutations of adjustments that have to be made to compensate. Instead of ten things to remember about a project when one has the right resources, there is a factorial addition of tasks to take into consideration.

Since employees usually have multiple projects, an organization with this chronic problem increases the workload of each employee, making each one far less productive, more frustrated, and unable to sufficiently satisfy the demands of clients. This piling-on effect eventually results in customers going elsewhere for the service they need.

When this problem occurs in government, it is especially grievous, because of government's monopolistic nature. Many people's worst nightmare is to need something critical that only government can provide, leaving them at the complete mercy of a bureaucrat.

Prognosis

If the organization turns a sufficient profit and obtains adequate resources, progress can be made at addressing the issues at hand. However, if insufficient or inadequate finances, personnel, or processes persist, unless the organization has a monopoly over the industry, customers will make other choices and the organization may eventually go out of business.

Treatment or Cure

- Make two lists: first, what resources one needs, and second, what resources one has. Make commitments based on the resources one has.
- Work at addressing and acquiring what you don't have. First, identify why you lack what is needed. Take the necessary actions to increase availability of resources. Start with the low-hanging fruit and immediately fix what is possible. This includes identifying and using unspent funds from other projects, reprioritizing organizational needs, applying for grants, and reorganizing for efficiency and process improvements.
- Appropriately address those employees who do not understand the importance of the survival of the organization or are not capable or committed to performing in a manner that maximizes return on investment.

Case Study

Turning a Blind Eye

An organization pulled itself out of bankruptcy by acquiring a sizeable loan that had to be paid back over several years. The annual payments were significant, requiring the company to cut back in a lot of important areas. Anything that wasn't mission critical was cut.

Ironically, one of the areas cut was the management auditing function that examined and recommended ways to improve the efficiency and effectiveness of operations. This function could have been used to do the analysis in determining where to make the necessary cuts after bankruptcy. Because the auditing function was discarded, for nearly fifteen years the organization operated without the benefit of independent performance audits that could have identified and brought about the implementation of needed cost-saving measures. As such, the efficiency and effectiveness of the organization's operations were highly dependent upon the self-motivation and skill sets of individual leaders and management. Highly motivated and skilled leaders ran solid operations. Those operating less efficiently cost the organization several millions of dollars over time as things progressively deteriorated, exacerbated by the knowledge that no one was monitoring their progress or holding them accountable.

Eventually, the organization reinstituted a skeleton audit function that produced substantial dividends, such as:

- reducing overtime costs
- improving IT strategic planning and the inventorying of IT assets
- improving land and building development processes, including improvements in customer service
- identifying strategies to save millions of dollars in the collective bargaining process
- identifying internal financial control weaknesses and inappropriate activities
- improving the risk management process

Misdiagnosis

Attributing the wrong causes and, as a result, implementing the wrong solutions to remedy an organizational deficiency.

Healthy and Normal Function

Company executives should have qualified in-house staff or contracted experts evaluate major organizational deficiencies and recommend solutions. The resulting recommendations should be reviewed by the proper individuals in the organization and consensus reached before making major resource allocations or changes to company processes or structure.

Causes of Dysfunction

- curing the symptom rather than the root cause
- taking a short-term view of the issue
- following the wrong advice
- not doing necessary homework
- lack of experience
- lack of humility
- having the wrong assumptions
- asking the wrong questions

Risk to the Organization

Making the right diagnosis the first time saves time and money. The risks of continued misdiagnosis include the opportunity cost of misdirecting scarce resources; sunk costs created by continuing on with the wrong diagnosis and treatment; damage to credibility by making an inaccurate diagnosis; and worsening of the deficiency due to application of the wrong cure.

Symptoms and Signs

- a deficiency that does not get better, or gets worse
- a diagnosis and subsequent treatment that creates a new problem
- a feeling of frustration from the "patient"

Diagnostic Analysis

This disease may be confirmed by the cure not working.

Progression and Impact

Generally, management diseases don't get the same kind of attention as medical diseases. For example, by law, society lets only credentialed doctors diagnose and treat medical diseases, yet for a variety of reasons, there are all kinds of noncredentialed staff who are allowed to opine on nearly any managerial issue. As a result, there is a whole lot of misdiagnosing going on, and the damage can be just as severe to an organization as it is to a living organism. The corporation is a legal entity that employs people and promotes the economic health of families. It's also not just the misdirection of resources involved, but the cost necessary to redirect those resources elsewhere once the misdiagnosis is discovered, as well as the opportunity cost of not being able to do something else that was critical.

The progression of this disease is highly dependent on who the organization allows to diagnosis management deficiencies. Is it an experienced and talented individual with a good track record or, is it the boss's third cousin?

Prognosis

If the job of diagnosing company deficiencies is limited to a talented few, most mistakes can be mitigated. However, if too many or the wrong people have access to the organizational heartbeat and shock paddles, the health of the organization can be in serious jeopardy.

Treatment or Cure

- Only allow the most talented to diagnose management deficiencies.
- Have a robust debate among qualified staff and reach consensus on issues that will result in major resource allocations.

Case Study

Training Wheel Trio

Ray, an inexperienced CEO, made several poor choices for C-suite personnel. When finished, Ray, along with two of his poorest choices, formed an inner circle that was surreptitiously dubbed the Training Wheel Trio. These individuals proceeded to diagnose organizational and management maladies that they were unqualified to assess.

Those with the proper experience at first tried to assist, and then as a last resort, to object, but were looked at as if they had three heads. As a result, Ray made a number of poor recommendations to the board of directors, which were quickly exposed. Rather than learn from the mistakes, Ray continued misdiagnosing various other issues. To make matters worse, he chastised and withheld rewards from those qualified personnel who tried to assist.

At the end of the day, the best and brightest fled, and millions of dollars were wasted. In the end, Ray even misdiagnosed himself, which resulted in an ignominious exit from the organization.

Observations and Final Comments

Thank you for wading into the ward of management diseases and disorders. We hope we haven't created any organizational hypochondriacs in the process. Indeed, we intend just the opposite. We wrote this book to provide healing opportunities for both employees and organizations. Our goal is to be a resource for looking up management diseases and disorders, properly identifying problems, and finding and implementing remedies to make organizational health a real and present benefit.

Writing this book has provided us with the opportunity to cogitate and analyze the information in its totality over time. From these reflections, we humbly proffer a few observations and conclusions for your consideration:

- Organizations are inanimate objects that cannot think, feel, or act. Those are human functions performed by the employees of the organization. As such, it is important to consider that nearly every disease or disorder, in some way, shape, or form, is substantially the result of a shortcoming in individual personalities or culture (the amalgamation of personalities). The most prolific personality and behavioral deficiencies noted during the compilation of *Management Diseases and Disorders* were ego, insecurity, accepting a job for which one lacks the appropriate skill set, manipulation, fear, a lack of respect for others, retaliatory behavior, inability to recognize truth that matches reality, and an overriding desire for self-interest.
- Each personality deficiency increases an employee's susceptibility to and often results in the acquisition of multiple diseases and disorders.
- It takes three parties to spread a management disease from its carrier: the employee with the disease, the organization that provides a vehicle for transmission, and its voluntary acceptance by another employee. When employees bring their personality shortcomings into the workplace, the organization can either intelligently address them or, by a lack of attention, give them free rein to metastasize.
- In many cases, there is a huge disparity between what organizations say they believe and how they actually operate. Office hallways and boardrooms are overcrowded with these unhealthy dissonances.
- Most employees want to work in a fair and just organization. However, for most, their primary objective is a paycheck to support their families. Leadership must proactively provide the means and modes of operation to develop an ethical organization, or it will not just happen on its own. Once the rules, for better or worse, are established, employees will adjust accordingly.

- Thinking well is integral to acting intelligently. Acting intelligently includes operating efficiently and effectively, which is at the heart of running a successful organization. According to James Sire, "Bias, preconceived erroneous ideas, hastily skipping over relevant details, having an inordinate desire for a preconceived outcome, fear of the implications of an idea, unwillingness to accept the consequences of correct reasoning: all of these and more stand in the way of the mind's reaching a worthy judgment."[12] Ergo, contrary to modern pluralistic belief, it matters what people think, as thoughts direct actions and have consequences for a great many people's lives and health, not just in the workplace.
- If we ever hope to operate worthy organizations, these diseases and disorders must be identified, understood, and treated. Failure to do so will shorten the life span of the organization and turn a going concern into one that's gone.
- Just as with our personal health, all managers will acquire one type of management disease or another at various points in their careers. Your best course of action is to pursue prevention, avoid the worst diseases, and identify and treat any disease we acquire as soon as possible.
- Unlike physical diseases, management diseases cannot be involuntarily given to us by others. We ultimately have the choice of whether or not we accept the disease.

So there you have it: Identify the problem. Admit to having it. Apply the right medicine. Your employees will appreciate it, and your bottom line will positively reflect it. Here's to a clean bill of organizational health!

Steve and Peter
June 2016

---

[12] James Sire, *Habits of the Mind* (Downers Grove, Illinois: InterVarsity Press, 2000), 84.

About the Authors

Peter and I came to know each other from our employment with the County of Orange in California. For a combined fifty-one years, we were practitioners and executives on the front lines of the county's multiple venues. The County of Orange serves the sixth-largest county populace in the United States with more than eighteen thousand employees and a $5.6 billion annual budget.

The significance of county government for many people is relatively obscure but critically important. Counties are the regional service providers for nearly every important aspect of daily living in areas like public safety (law enforcement, district attorney / public defender, courts, probation), social services (welfare, child protection), health care (mental health, disease prevention, correctional medical), recreational services (parks and beaches), personal services (birth/marriage/ death certificates, real estate transactions, property taxes), transportation (airport, roads, harbors), voting, and public works (flood control, waste management, permits and licensing, construction).

Providing these critical services in a public sector environment is a constant challenge, particularly with five term-limited elected officials being in charge. Sometimes there are high fives (votes), low fives, or no fives. Sometimes there are three high fives and two low fives. At other times, there are sharpened knives and running for one's lives.

For eighteen years, Dr. Hughes served as Orange County's internal audit director, performing financial, control, and operational audits of each of the county's twenty-four departments. In addition, the internal audit department ran the fraud hotline, which received and investigated all manner of spoof and nonfiction related to waste, fraud, and abuse. The nonfiction claims (those that were substantiated) represented approximately 10 to 15 percent of all allegations, but they were doozies, ranging from sexual abuse to contracting and political scandals.

Dr. Hughes previously worked for the Jet Propulsion Laboratories in Pasadena, the University of Oregon, CBS, and Arthur Anderson in auditing and financial roles. In 2010, Dr. Hughes was voted CPA of the Year for Local Governmental Agencies by the American Institute of Certified Public Accountants. Additionally, he coauthored the Association of Certified Fraud Examiners' 2009 Article of the Year, "Ethics Pays in So Many Ways." Currently, Dr. Hughes is an Assistant Auditor-Controller for Los Angeles County, the largest populated county in the United States. He also periodically serves as an Associate Professor in local universities.

Academically, Peter earned his Ph.D. in Administration from Oregon State University, a Masters of Business Administration from the University of California at Riverside, and a Bachelor's degree in Moral and Ethical Philosophy from Pomona College. Peter also holds the following certifications: Certified Public Accountant, Certified Internal Auditor, Certified Information

Technology Professional, Certified Fraud Examiner, Certified Compliance and Ethics Professional, Certified Financial Forensics, and Chartered Global Management Accountant.

Over my thirty-three years at the county, I held a number of varied posts and obtained multiple "passports": chief human resources officer, performance audit director, director of administration for a variety of departments, chief of organizational assessment/development, and the high-wire frontline jobs of regional landfill manager and go-to personnel investigator, just to name a few. It should also be noted that I am a survivor of the county's 1994 bankruptcy, which at the time was the largest municipal bankruptcy in US history.

In my assignments from the shop floor to the C-suite, I spent time, in one form or another, in nearly every functional area of the county. For my work in performance audit, the county was awarded Harvard's highly competitive Kennedy School / Ash Center for Democratic Government and Innovation 2012 "Bright Ideas" recognition. Academically, I earned a Masters of Business & Public Administration, and a Bachelor's degree in Political Science from the University of California at Irvine (UCI). I also serve as a Lecturer at UCI, teaching a "Business & Government" class. In the private sector, I worked for United Parcel Service (UPS) and the Dr. Pepper Bottling Company, which I thank for helping to finance my college education. Additionally, I was a thirty-year NCAA and high school basketball referee.

In these varied leadership roles, Dr. Hughes and I have endeavored to do the right thing for the right reason in service to our employer and the public. This approach was variously rewarded and punished over the years, depending upon the quality of leadership in power at the time. We often wondered what benefits would result from working for an organization with the highs of Everest and the lows of Marianas Trench. From Everest came the mentoring; from Mariana came baptisms by fire.

The outcomes of our experiences were many times so palpable that they have been seared into our consciences. It's hard to forget the glories of the truth overcoming the corporate powers that be and their political manipulations, and the deep valleys of seeing personal ambition win the day (but not the battle). We have truly witnessed the best and worst a large organization has to offer. Perhaps our experiences will be valuable to others as we try to identify and find cures for what ails the corporate soul and its key players.